CW01283376

How I Failed to Save The World

Or Forty Years of Foreign Aid

by

GORDON BRIDGER

A witty, humorous, perceptive, personal account of living and working in the Rhodesias, Ethiopia, Chile, Bolivia, Paraguay, the Maldives, Tonga, Gilbert and Ellice Islands, Australia, and many other developing countries over a period of forty years

authorHOUSE®

AuthorHouse™ UK Ltd.
500 Avebury Boulevard
Central Milton Keynes, MK9 2BE
www.authorhouse.co.uk
Phone: 08001974150

©*2008 Gordon Bridger. All rights reserved.*

No part of this book may be reproduced, stored in a retrieval system, or transmitted by any means without the written permission of the author.

First published by AuthorHouse 7/2/2008

ISBN: 978-1-4343-9445-3 (sc)

Printed in the United States of America
Bloomington, Indiana

This book is printed on acid-free paper.

Acknowledgements

I am particularly grateful to Chris Farara without whose insistence and editorial help I might not have completed this work. I must also thank Jean, my long suffering wife of over 40 years who frequently had to interrupt her good works and crossword puzzles to read early drafts, as well as Matthew Alexander, Stephen Hodgart and Margaret Hill whose corrections and insights helped me immensely. I am also deeply grateful to the very many people, starting with my parents and Cousin April, and many others, who have helped me throughout my life.

Preface

Many of us as children will recall being chastised by our parents for not eating at mealtimes by reminders of "starving Chinese children".

The consequences of such childhood exhortations can have surprising results. In my case it was a factor which nearly led to me running a 10,000-ton ship aground in the Atlantic, studying at the London School of Economics and being blacklisted by MI5 for writing an article in the communist Daily Worker, in advising racist farmers in what was then Southern Rhodesia, and having my wife drive through the streets of Addis Ababa waving a white pillow case with UN marked on it during a revolution. It was an important consideration in fulfilling an adolescent dream of joining the United Nations, living through earthquakes in that garden of Eden, Chile, travelling on death-defying roads in the high Bolivian Andes. It led to becoming Director of Economics of all the British Government's country-aid programmes, having a two-hour-long audience with the King of Tonga, visiting the fabled Gilbert and Ellice Islands and the underwater coral paradise of the Maldive Islands long before the tourists got there; buying a 1.5 million acre ranch in Australia for the Sultan of Brunei, being elected Mayor of Guildford in 2003 and finally ending up, like Candide in Voltaire's social satire, cultivating pumpkins on my allotment in Guildford.

CONTENTS

Chapter 1	Goodbye Buenos Aires	1
Chapter Two	White Africa	11
Chapter Three	An African Empire	33
Chapter Four	The Last Country In The World	67
Chapter Five	Back To England	93
Chapter Six	How I Met The King Of Tonga	103
Chapter Seven	The Road Of Death - Bolivia	133
Chapter Eight	A Very Unusual Conference	149
Chapter Nine	Mission To The Maldives	155
Chapter Ten	Rise And Fall	163
Chapter Eleven	A "Station" For The Sultan	177
Chapter Twelve	Mayor Of Guildford	185
Chapter Thirteen	Reflections	197

Chapter 1

GOODBYE BUENOS AIRES

In 1948 the port of Buenos Aires was a real port. Ships from all over the world made their way up the brown muddy waters of the River Plate to one of the great grain and meat exporting docks of the world. It bustled ,with cranes loading the ships, with sweating exploited dock workers bent double under huge sacks of grain, while drunken sailors tottered around, and the bars were full of ladies with over painted faces shouting " Hi Jonny you like -- -- ?"

As a bored nineteen-year-old Anglo-Argentine there was a vicarious pleasure entailed in visiting what was regarded as an "out of bounds" part of Buenos Aires. On a visit to the docks it occurred to me that one of these ships might provide the means of escape from boredom to a more exciting world in the USA or Britain. Boredom is not a word that tourists would associate with the exotic late nineteenth-century baroque centre of Buenos Aires with its parks and hundreds of superb restaurants.

Even making allowance for adolescent frustrations, the problem was (and is) that the huge " island" conurbation of Buenos Aires with its teeming millions, is a mass of mainly bleak undistinguished buildings isolated by the muddy waters of the River Plate on one side and by hundreds of miles of flat endless Pampas on the other. It was not, and is not, easy to get away to a different environment, even for the rich. Admittedly there were, and are, many fine leafy suburbs and many sporting facilities but these do not overcome a sense of urban isolation.

I was born in Buenos Aires. My parents were of English and Scottish descent, though they had been born in Uruguay. I had been to a private English school and left at the age of sixteen with reasonable educational qualifications and took a job, as was the norm for most Anglo-Argentine youths, with a large British petroleum company. The work was incredibly boring for as a "trainee" my work entailed filing letters which I usually misfiled and then could not find when requested to do so. This seemed to irritate my superiors. Some escape from this tedium was provided by jokes the "juniors" played on each other, the principal one being covering the telephone earpiece of a colleague with sticky glue and then telephoning him.

Life was made tolerable by weekends at the various British country clubs where one got rid of one's frustrations playing rugby, cricket, tennis or swimming and during evenings when one went to dances with pretty young soft-breasted girls whose virtue was just added to one's adolescent frustrations.

Faced with an endless career of mis-administration in this large petroleum company I decided to explore opportunities to see the world. What about a job on one of those ships?

My first attempts to secure a job on the ships themselves were frustrated as I was chased off the ones I boarded by unfriendly crew who said I was trespassing, or by being told that the Captain was not there. I then met a friend who knew someone in the British Consulate who said that they would introduce to me a ship's Captain.

It was thus that I met Captain X. He was a short and elegantly dressed figure with several stripes on his uniform. "Excuse me Sir," I said as politely and respectfully as I could, "any chance of a job on your ship on your return to England?" It never occurred to me to ask myself what qualifications I had for this task. Fortunately it never occurred to him to ask me either.

He looked me up and down, presumably counting arms and legs and asking what sports I played and then, much to my surprise he said "Yes – I can take you on as a Deck Boy." I was not really expecting an offer but hid my shock and replied very politely "That's brilliant Sir. What does a Deck Boy do?" I asked very politely.

"You will be on the Dog Watch – 4 o'clock to 8 o'clock, twice a day. Two hours on watch – two hours steering."

Did I hear right? "Two Hours watching" sounded as if it was something I could do, but 'steering'! I had never been to sea, could not steer a car and the only time I had been rowing I had broken an oar. Was he crazy? Me steer a 10,000- ton ship which had a crew of 45 who might perish if I got it wrong?

Instead of refusing his offer I heard myself saying "When do we leave Sir?"

"Two weeks from to-day" he replied.

My family and friends were startled by my new career, my older brothers thinking I was demented, or the Captain was, and my relieved employers did not object at all to my sudden resignation.

S.S. ELSTREE GRANGE

The great day came. I was shown a cabin which had only two feet between bunks and accommodated four of us in a space which seemed more appropriate for a slave ship.

My responsibilities got off to a good start. As we passed a rusty Uruguayan naval vessel I was thrilled to be told to go and lower the flag as sign of respect. I did this and even saluted smartly, much to the amazement of several idle Uruguayan sailors, as we glided past.

I was then asked if I would work overtime. This seemed an excellent idea since it would add to my wages. My first overtime task entailed chipping off rusty paint. This required me hitting, for hours on end, odd bits of the ship. Iron chips flew off and I wondered how long it would take before there was nothing left of it. It was very boring. At 10 am I was told to go off for a tea break. The mess room was empty and having served myself some tea I found about fifteen beautiful sugary doughnuts in the refrigerator. I ate five of them. Then the other seamen came down for tea - fourteen of them. "Who's the b – who's eaten my dough nut" shouted one, and then the others followed. I uttered not a word. To this day I feel guilty.

Next day out of the main sea lanes I was taken up to the wheelhouse. There was an internal covered wheelhouse but this second one was further up, exposed to the elements as the Captain was not going to have softies steering his ship. We were protected however, by a five foot high wooden wall which enabled us to see where we going and gave us some protection from the wind.

The Mate showed me what I had to do. I had to stand at the helm, a large steering wheel, and make sure the ship followed the compass direction of North East. It seemed quite simple in the passive flat sea on which we were slowly making our way. I moved the wheel slightly to the left. It moved to the left. I tried it gently to the right and I was off course. I thought I better not experiment too much or it might upset the Captain. It really was very simple. Nothing to it.

After about 10 minutes I started to get bored. When the First Mate also got bored and confident that I would not cause too much chaos he left me on my own. I wondered what would happen if I took my hands off the wheel? I did. Nothing happened. The ship ploughed on. I did more testing to see how long I could keep my hands off the wheel before it went too far off course. I would get to about three minutes before I had to bring it round again. For the first hour or so the ship veered a bit from side to side but not enough to cause any comment.

On my next watch I was more relaxed and found myself getting bored again. I started doing exercises. I realised I could run round the wheelhouse and leave the ship to steer itself. On one occasion I unfortunately stopped to look over the side and found myself staring into the Captain's face. He seemed astonished, "Who's at the wheel?" he bellowed. He did not seem to realise that the ship could perfectly well steer itself for short periods of time. I rushed back and shouted "All under control Sir."

On another all too quietly boring steering watch I drifted around and, peering down one of those large ventilators which come up from the bowels of the ship, I put my head into it and shouted "Wakey wakey, shipmates all on deck" or something equally stupid, and was shocked to hear coming in reply a string of quite foul language from the Captain, the ventilator was for his cabin, was over his bunk and he had been sleeping – at 7 pm too.

I always seemed to be getting into trouble for the most trivial of errors. During my overtime I was told to paint the outside of the galley with white paint. I am a very fast worker and in no time I had finished all the wooden bits and decided that the wire netting which went round it should be painted. On completion the chief cook came in to examine my handiwork. He went berserk. He had foolishly left all his buns and bread on a shelf on the others side of the netting and they were decorated with little white spots. He did not even laugh when I offered to scrape them off

My relations with him then got even worse as he was stupidly standing looking over the side of the ship while smoking a cigarette downwind from me when I emptied a bucket of slops over the side. Naturally a lot of it was blown all over him – I did not offer to clean him up but fled before he had time to catch me.

I do not think my brain could have been working all that well for one of my jobs was to go around and wake the more senior crew at 6 am every morning. I was a sort of a mobile clock and had to shake up about ten crew. One morning they refused to wake up and I really had to shout and pummel them to get to work. When I got back on watch I realised I had woken them all at 5am. I rushed back pushing them back into their bunks and putting out their lights. I hate to think what they said about me at breakfast.

I should have realised that something might go wrong when, during my chats with the First Mate who was in charge of my watch, I was surprised to discover that my knowledge of astronomy was greater than his. On dark nights in the southern hemisphere the sky can be dazzlingly beautiful and so as a curious youth I had learned the names of most stars – and was able to point them out to him: Sirius, Canopus, Alpha Centauri, Beta Centauri, all splendid names. He seemed interested and impressed.

As we went further north the stars disappeared and the early mornings were bleak, dark and cloudy and I frequently regretted leaving home. One early black morning when I was on lonely watch at the wheel the visibility was exceptionally poor. It was very cold and I wished I was at home tucked up in bed wwhen a huge cloud appeared before us and I could almost feel the rain pouring down. Then with a rush the Mate appeared. He was shouting using very strong language which due to my genteel middle class upbringing I was not used to and found most distasteful. The substance of his abuse was that he wanted me to alter course, and quickly. This is what I assumed "hard a starboard" meant. It sounded splendidly nautical and I was doing this when he wrenched the wheel from me and went quite mad turning the ship around. It did a complete U turn within a few seconds. This was fortunate for the clouds I was expecting to drench us turned out to be a massive mountain which had appeared from nowhere out of the black ocean. As we turned I saw white breakers only about a couple of hundred yards away. The Cape Verde Islands had somehow got in our path.

I often wonder what would have happened if I had continued on course. I could imagine my elder brothers would have said to my mother: "Typical! You should have known better than to let him loose". Or maybe the tabloid press would run a headline "Deck Boy runs ship aground – 45 lives lost."

Mercifully this did not happen but interestingly enough no one told me off. After all I was on course and it was the Mate who had set it. I often wonder whether I may have misinformed him about the position of Alpha Centauri.

A few cold dark days later we were approaching England and rounded Ireland to land at Liverpool where I was, much to my and no doubt everyone else's relief, taken off the wheel as we approached the Mersey River. The outline of Liverpool was forbiddingly depressing from the docks. When I was signed off at Liverpool and I lined up to get my discharge certificate I wondered how the First Mate, who was sitting at the desk paying us off, would stamp it. He stamped it "Very Good". He laughed loudly as he did so.

My wage packet was based on pay of £7 18s per month, yes, per month. Plus 105 hours of overtime at 1s 3d per hour. I had earned a useful £14 10s 6d for 34 days work and had made it to England.

BRITAIN

It was a dark cold January evening as four of us crew commandeered a taxi at the docks As we piled in an experienced colleague collected five shillings from each us to give " the copper at the gate a quid – otherwise the f- b- will hold us up and search all our baggage". Such was my introduction to British Police who I thought I knew about from descriptions of the friendly policeman in middle- class P.G.Wodehouse's novels and from accounts in the Illustrated London News. The £1 bribe was quite a lot in those days – one seventh of my monthly wage as a Deck Boy, and maybe £50 today.

After a few days in London, I spent the next six months hitchhiking first round Britain and then, with a pleasant amiable Australian lad, Ross, even more naive than myself, round Europe. Since the £35 I had saved did not last long our travels were punctuated by spells of work in warehouses, farms, and restaurants.

Britain, with its gothic churches and Tudor buildings, was a splendid revelation which those brought up in the country take for granted, but a "foreigner" could enjoy much more. Youth hostels provided a cheap and friendly refuge from Land's End to John O'Groats.

With Ross I decided to visit Sweden where we believed we would find a model society and friendly girls. Our journey there took us through the still devastated German cities of Hamburg and Bremen. Not a single tall building had survived the ravages of bombing – an endless vista of urban scarecrows. Guernica writ large. Did they deserve this Armageddon?

Sweden was a disappointment. Stockholm was modern but dull, the girls very unfriendly, though a job in a restaurant enabled us to replenish our weakened physiques which had had to survive on a budget of five shillings a day.

We decided to head south for warmer friendlier climes, stopping over to sell our blood in Switzerland, where we were paid five shillings per 100 centilitres. To Ross's annoyance they could only squeeze 300 from my weakened body, while he gave 500. .

This kept us going for a few days until we landed up at the tiny French Riviera port of St Tropez. The dazzling translucent "Raoul Duffy" blue sea set against a coast of pine trees lulled by the buzz of cicadas was the closest to paradise we had come. In 1949 there were no tourists, just a couple of large lazy yachts in the harbour surrounded by small shady empty quayside cafes and bars.

Funds were running out and a job was urgent. It was close to the end of summer and the large Arab owner of a Chateau, with a vineyard full of grapes which needed harvesting, was looking for workers. He was fussy about whom he chose as he had five, yes five, unattached daughters and he was not having any Frenchmen around them. He would say "Je n'ai pas d' enfants – seulement cinq jeunes filless". However, one man's bad luck can be others good fortune.

We spent three weeks cutting and squashing grapes – my job, between listening to the melancholy beauty of his daughters, who had been pressed into grape harvesting, singing" La Vie en Rose" and having grape fights with them, entailed bashing the grapes into large barrels. Our employer, who was one of the dimmest individuals I had come across, said of me when he thought I could not hear " Il est fort – mais il est bête.". On balance, a compliment. I liked the "fort" bit.

The chateau fringed a beautiful, sandy, blue sea, beach where we adjourned after work. We were the only ones on this paradise, except on one happy occasion when a single naked beauty walked past, politely putting her hands over her breasts as she did so. Now the beach, Plage Pamplonne, is one of the most popular overcrowded semi- nude beaches on the Riviera.

As autumn set in we hitched our way back to London. What to do next? Go home to Argentina? Go back to my old job? No way. Fortunately I had discovered a splendidly hospitable cousin living with her large family in Hampstead Garden Suburb and I discussed my dilemma with her.

"Why don't you study economics?," she suggested, "there are evening courses you could take".

Since I had no independent source of income or savings evening study was the only solution. I would have to work at the same time. I had thought it would be interesting to study psychology or archaeology though the first seemed rather introspective and the second unlikely to lead to a job. Economics sounded interesting to an awakening social conscience.

"Where could I do that" I asked?

"You could try the London School of Economics" she replied.

"I want to go to a University, not back to school," I replied.

"It is a University," she said, "Professor Laski teaches there".

Now that sounded interesting. I had heard of him for he was a famous Socialist who seemed to know all the answers to the world and its economic problems. I could sit at his feet and learn to solve them. Then on graduation, I could join the United Nations and do something about all those starving Chinese children I had been told about. My career was settled.

So next day I went into London and to the London School of Economics. It was a great disappointment, just a huge office block with a tiny grubby cafe outside it. No medieval spires, no green lawns to walk around on. Still I decided to give it a chance and asked a helpful lady at a counter how I could register? Alas my school examination results were not sufficient. I would need to take another entrance exam to get in. She seemed to think I could do this quite easily in a few months at the Regent Street Polytechnic. Then I could become a student at the LSE.

"Well," I thought, "beggars can't be choosers," and I decided to follow her advice.

Four years later, thanks to many part-time jobs and a helpful cousin, I graduated as an economist at the LSE. Much to my surprise I kept being turned down for all the worthy public sector jobs I applied for. Discreet enquiries revealed that my left- wing views, Socialist rather than Communist, combined with the fact that I had written an article for the Communist Daily Worker about an anarchist trial in Spain which I had attended as an interpreter for the Labour Party Observer, combined with a report from one of my LSE Tutors, had got me in the bad books of M I5 and they thought I was a threat to the State. So I delayed my applications and took a post- graduate M.A. at Manchester University in Agricultural Economics. Then without those who had sought to blemish a brilliant career knowing about it, I secured a job in Africa.

The rest, or some of the more interesting parts, is my story.

Chapter Two

WHITE AFRICA

As I drove round a sharp bend on a dirt road, leaving a huge cloud of brown dust in my wake, a startled Kudu, a sort of antelope as large as a mature cow, stood blocking my path. Startled, it rose gracefully and fortunately speedily into the air, as if propelled by elastic, and disappeared into the bush. While I was resting in the car after several hours of dusty driving, a troop of curious baboons surrounded it examining its occupant. One jumped on the bonnet and peered at me through the windscreen.

I was on my first professional job, visiting European farmers in the highlands of Central Africa. Far away and long ago they were part of Southern Rhodesia. We were at 5,000 feet above sea level on a great level grassy plain studded with acacia trees and tall grey eucalyptus where European farmers had established themselves. How on earth had I ended up here?

I had been appointed, in 1957, as an Economist to the Ministry of Agriculture in the now defunct Federation of Rhodesia and Nyasaland. The Federation had been created in 1953, but was wound up at the end of 1963 after the famous "wind of change" speech by the then Prime Minister, Harold MacMillan, in Cape Town in 1960, which led to Britain's too hasty abandonment of its African colonies. The high cost of maintaining them and the pressures for independence abruptly tipped the balance in favour of decolonisation.

This new Federation was an administrative attempt to tidy up the three responsibilities Britain had in Central Africa. There was a dynamic self-governing European run colony in Southern Rhodesia, a prosperous copper- producing colony in Northern Rhodesia and a small impoverished tea- producing colony in Nyasaland.

The Federal government was firmly in the hands of Europeans but with some African representation, though in no way did it reflect either demographic reality or the economic contribution of the copper producing Northern Rhodesia The decision to establish a Federation was much disliked by articulate Africans in the two northern territories but it was pushed through despite this opposition, by the British Government. There were plans to liberalise and democratise the Federation over time and to get rid of the many racially discriminatory laws in Southern Rhodesia. It was the intention, unlike that of the apartheid regime in South Africa, that the Federation should be a liberal African democracy.

This was undoubtedly, looking back, a naïve hope, but one which attracted the naïve. I was one of them.

On graduation from University I had applied for several jobs in the British Civil Service, including the Colonial Office, but they all refused to employ me. I was deemed a security threat – having been at the London School of Economics and reported by one of my tutors as having "strong left wing views" to M I5, an assessment not entirely untrue but the reactions, so I thought, far exceeded my danger to society. I suppose I should add that I had written an article in the Communist Daily Worker about the iniquities of a trial in Franco's Spain of anarchists who had tried to blow up a cement mixer in the factory that Evita Peron was visiting, in Barcelona in 1952, and which the Labour observer, the famous Peter Benenson (he founded Amnesty International), who attended the trial, was not prepared to write. How was I involved? I went as his interpreter as I spoke Spanish.

So I applied for a job in the newly formed Federation. Africa sounded exciting, a salary of £1,000 a year was almost twice as much as I would have been paid in Britain and there were much better chances of a challenging and interesting job. Incredibly, looking back, such was the faith in this new society, that recruits were not offered "home" leave. Africa was to be our new home. Meanwhile, and fortunately, M1-5 had been remiss in informing the new Federal Government of my dangerous background and they happily recruited me, unaware of the danger they faced. When MI-5 discovered my whereabouts, a year so later, after "interrogation" by the head of the local Public Service, they sensibly decided not to pursue me further.

GETTING THERE

The journey out, leaving Southampton one grey February day in 1957, was an experience which those who now fly to Africa in a few hours crushed into a precarious aluminium tube, and fed from tiny trays of plastic food, will sadly never experience.

Our Union Castle liner was full of young lively passengers – most going out to South Africa, the more daring to Central Africa. We had two weeks of splendid comfort, with games, fancy dress parties, much drinking and a fabulous stopover at Madeira which was a tropical paradise of colour and sunshine and cheap port.

In Cape Town a train awaited to take us on the three-day journey to the highlands of central Africa. Our sleeping compartments were comfortable and huge baskets of Cape fruit accompanied us as the train made its laborious way northward. First we had to be pulled up by a diesel locomotive over such geography-book features as the Great Karroo plateau which separates the fertile vine growing Cape Area from the mineral-rich areas of the Transvaal. Once over them a steam locomotive took over and we rolled through such painful historic names as Mafeking before reaching the endless relentless dry deserts of Botswana. Tiny naked children optimistically waved bananas and wooden souvenirs as the train resolutely made its way to the newly established Federation.

The first sight of the Federation consisted of the bleak bare cattle lands of the low veldt (grasslands) of Southern Rhodesia with its spiky acacias, sparse bush and baobab trees whose thick wide water-collecting trunks sprouted short thin water -saving finger like branches. But gradually as we climbed to the 5,000-foot plateau of the temperate cooler climate of the high veldt, the trees were more frequent, the grass more welcoming, there were green hills on the horizon and rain had recently fallen, transforming an early morning arrival into a splendid Arcadian panorama. The air was fresh, the sun warm and the sky blue

Salisbury – now Harare – named in the nineteenth century after the Foreign Secretary of the time, in the vain hope, no doubt, of loosening the purse strings of an ever-stingy British Treasury, was developing as an attractive modern European town. Broad avenues, with some tall new elegant buildings, a shopping street of European-owned shops with Edwardian arcades and wide avenues with purple jacaranda trees, attractive green parks, flowering gardens, created a dynamic centre of British social and economic achievement.

Those of us working for the Government, about twenty, were met at the station and taken out to a barely refurbished RAF airfield composed of long corrugated- iron- roof sheds divided into large bleak bedrooms with a large equally bleak canteen some ten miles from the capital. Though isolated, this rudimentary accommodation (largely male, as the plentiful female company on the ship dispersed once we arrived at Cape Town and later Salisbury) was perfectly adequate for "pioneer "youths such as ourselves. We consoled ourselves with locally produced lager beer and a splendid recording which I had wisely brought with me of Richard Burton in "Under Milk Wood".

EUROPEANS

At the time there were about 250,000 Europeans and over 5 million Africans in the Federation. Almost all the Europeans were in Southern Rhodesia. While Southern Rhodesia was a white self-governing colony, Northern Rhodesia and Nyasaland were under the amiable rule of the Colonial Office with panoply of District Commissioners, Provincial Commissioners and Governors with pomp, protocol and plumed hats.

European settlement was scarcely many decades old and it had only been sixty years earlier that the last two African slave traders in northern Nyasaland had been captured and summarily shot by the District Commissioner who, with a handful of Indian Sepoys, had captured them. No international tribunals in those days. And it was hardly 50 years since the first Europeans had settled in the south and put down uprisings by the resentful Matabele and Mashona tribes who were not at all keen on their lands being taken over by a flood of white settlers.

Racial discrimination was widespread only in the south and was strongest in those areas where a European working class thought, correctly, that African advancement would be at their expense. Nevertheless it was not entrenched as firmly as it was in South Africa and from time to time slow steps were taken towards removing many of the more irksome racial restrictions. But Africans were not allowed into European hotels, cinemas and bars and were not allowed to live in European designated areas – except as employees. This was a white man's Africa.

The economy of the Federation was benefiting from the post- war boom thanks to copper exports from the north, agricultural exports and chrome from the south and tea and other plantation crops from Nyasaland.

EUROPEAN FARMING

European owned land accounted for an astonishing 42% of all of Southern Rhodesia – and was distributed amongst only 6,000 white farmers. The low dry veldt areas of the south and west were extremely unproductive and cattle production was the only source of income. Farming could only be carried out profitably by Europeans on farms of tens of thousands of acres. In the much more productive high veldt, the main focus of settlement and production, the average farm was closer to 5,000 acres but probably less than 20% of this land was ever farmed. The Eastern Highlands, reminiscent of the most beautiful parts of Western Scotland, but warmer and drier, allowed for temperate fruits in the higher areas, and tropical fruits in the lower warmer valleys.

The Economics Department I joined consisted of seven youngish and pleasant Europeans based in a rambling corrugated shed under spacious delightful eucalyptus trees imported from Australia many years before. Its head was an extremely able British trained PhD, and the Deputy a very bright Cambridge graduate whose father had been a failed Ecuadorian revolutionary and had taken refuge in Britain where he had married an English girl.

One of the earliest lessons I learned from him was when our Minister, being concerned about farmers' low incomes, asked that a report be produced to show how they could be increased. This was given to me to produce. When I handed in my report to my boss which concluded that farmers' incomes had gone up substantially and I could not see a reason for an increase in farm prices to help them he called me in and said "Are you mad ? The Minister wants to increase farm incomes" I protested feebly but was cut short by his advice "You can say a glass of water is half full, or half empty. Go away and think about it again." Lo and behold I went away and thought about it again and concluded that farmers incomes had not gone up nearly as much as others had.

My first major responsibility entailed touring the country to collect from farmers their financial data about their incomes and costs of production. This data enabled the Government to set guaranteed prices for farm output, or at least for those crops whose marketing they could control. It was widely agreed by us professionals and politicians at least, that the inherent instability of farm production led to so much price fluctuation that investment levels were severely restricted unless some sort of price guarantees were offered to farmers. A secondary, but important benefit of farm costs was that farmers could compare their expenditure, yields and income with those of other farmers and learn from the most efficient.

The most profitable and prevalent crops grown by farmers were Virginia flue- cured tobacco and maize. Both of these crops were produced on a large scale and required considerable skill and effort, particularly the former, and they also needed significant financial investment.

The upside of my assignment was that I was immediately provided with a loan to purchase a brand new Opel station wagon. I had never had even a second- hand car before, and was confidently (and rightly) assured by my colleagues that I could easily repay the loan from my car travel allowance.

The downside was that I knew nothing about farming. I had worked on a dairy farm in England for a week, and chased stray cattle around my uncle's ranch in Argentina, but all my life had been spent in large cities. However my task was to extract financial information from farmers, not tell them how to run their business.

Driving around the savannah regions of this attractive part of the world, particularly in retrospect, was a pretty good assignment especially in a car which would eventually be mine if I clocked up enough mileage. This was very likely as the distances between farms were vast. It could take an hour's driving to get to another farm. We were on a huge plain at 5,000 feet above sea level, with a generally temperate climate, plenty of sunshine and never too hot. One often came across wild life in the shape of impalas, gazelle, kudus and baboons.

Most of the roads were dirt, often rattling one's car with their corrugations. However this could be overcome if one skimmed over them at 70 mph. It was extremely frustrating having to drive behind another vehicle as the dust raised by it totally obscured the road. It meant that passing the car in front entailed driving through a cloud of dust with zero visibility for several seconds. Overtaking was dangerously exciting as a vehicle might be coming the other way – a sort of Russian roulette of the road.

However, with luck one might travel on two narrow tarmac strips only one wheel wide built in the pre war depression, which one had to precariously to share with oncoming traffic. Deciding when to leave one of the strips to a vehicle made driving more interesting. Even more so if the oncoming vehicle was a large African- driven lorry. If this were the case it was prudent to leave both strips to it.

The hotels one stayed at were splendid rambling timbered buildings of the 1930s with creaking floors, huge verandas, cane furniture and sepia photographs in the dining rooms, in which one was served six-course meals by innumerable black staff. The bar was frequented by local athletic- looking European farmers in khaki shorts and open shirts discussing farm prices or the inefficiency of their "boys". These were European- only hotels.

My visits gave me an opportunity to meet a wide range of farmers. The visits were always unexpected but they were usually quite pleased to see a new white face, even one as obviously fresh and citified as mine, and were prepared to sit down to go through their accounts and help me produce a financial statement. We would later send them average data from other farmers so they could compare yields and expenditure on different items such as labour and fertiliser, to see what they could learn from each other.

Most of the farmers were young bronzed and British in their 30s and 40s who had served in the war and had some form of secondary education, and had been tempted by Government incentives to see what they could make of farming. Determined and dynamic they had all the abilities of a "does it yourself" generation. They were typical of the many who have flourished in Britain as small- scale entrepreneurs. Most of them had a demonic energy and ability to create something out of very little. If Margaret Thatcher in later years ever wondered where to find British enterprise and initiative, well here it was transforming central Africa

Most farmers would employ between 30 and 50 "boys". In general the European farmers found it difficult to do other than look down on their labour who, used to the less demanding traditions of subsistence agriculture, often found working under demanding wage conditions confusing and excessive. Most Europeans complained of having to provide continual supervision to ensure work was satisfactory. It was impossible to say to what extent workers were ill treated. As a general rule the better educated and more prosperous the farmer, the better the labour force was treated. I came across some who provided schools and a shop for their workers but at the other extreme there were stories of ill treatment - although since there were no laws which forced labour to stay on a farm intelligent farmers had an interest in treating labour well .

In the south of the country there were a large number of Boer farmers who had migrated from South Africa and scraped a living from the these very dry lands. The young Boers harboured a grudge towards the British arising from their parents' treatment during the Boer war (one British historian said "The only people treated badly by the British in Africa were the Boers").This showed when I called on them as they were barely polite. On the other hand elderly Boer farmers were kindness personified. However the dual side of their personality came out when a large elderly Boer farmer commanded "You stay the night" He was a towering figure who regaled me with stories in imperfect English about their great trek northwards and how they had struggled to develop their rambling farm. In the morning he said "Boy - you come with me – I will show you my tobacco fields". As we left the farm house I could not believe my eyes as he picked up a long six- foot whip. Was he going to use it in front of me? What would I do if he did? Would I wrestle it from his grip? Would I explain to him that "Sorry Sir, it is against the law to beat your labour" and grab the whip from him? Oops, I was out of my depth. As we approached the tobacco fields where his "boys" were picking tobacco leave they suddenly saw him and I recall their eyes widening with fear. Fortunately he saw no need to lash out and I was spared any heroic gesture.

This was the only potentially unpleasant incident I came across in a year spent criss-crossing European farming areas .There were occasional reports of ill treatment by farmers of their labour force in the newspapers and the Courts would normally act against labour abuse.

The support system which farmers had in the form of agricultural advice, conservation advice, credit, research and marketing was impressive. Almost all practised forms of soil conservation, far in advance of most farmers in the world. There were large research stations for all the major crops; there were Marketing Boards for many of them, and a Farmers' Cooperative system to support their interests. Probably nearly half of the farmers were of world class standard, adopting best practice from counterparts in Australia, USA and Britain.

The most productive crop was Virginia flue cured tobacco, which, however, would only grow on sandy soils and required considerable investment in large curing sheds and skilled management to ensure quality tobacco resulted. Maize, grown on rich red soils using pioneering hybrids, achieved some of the highest yields of maize in the world.

The average farmer with, as mentioned earlier, around 5,000 acres of land, had more land than necessary. A tobacco farmer might grow 150 acres per year and allowing for rotation should easily have got by with half this amount of land. Maize farmers required more land but 5,000 acres was still far more than necessary for them.

However, in those days nearly 50 years ago, the European farmer was far from wealthy. he average farmer one would visit would have built himself a basic three or four- bedroomed house made of unplastered bricks with a corrugated iron roof and a wide "stoop" or veranda. All owned at least one tractor, and usually an aged car and lorry.

As an ex LSE "leftie," visiting the farmers was an interesting social experience, for one had to listen to their racial ranting with impassive patience. However one had to respect and indeed admire the way through sheer hard work, using modern technology, they had transformed this long neglected part of Africa.

My work soon extended into more interesting analytical work entailing regional surveys and evaluation of such products as bananas, sheep and pig production. Indeed I hit the headlines in the local paper for forecasting a pig surplus. This upset no end of pig farmers as everyone, except pig farmers, knows there is an inevitable pig "cycle" of surpluses and shortages. At various times I had been sent up to Northern Rhodesia where there were a few hundred white farmers along the "line of rail," and another small distressed group of elderly pioneer farmers stranded near the Nyasaland frontier in the beautiful but remote Fort Jameson whose problems I was supposed to help resolve.

NORTHERN RHODESIA

I was eventually transferred to Lusaka, the capital, where I was the sole representative of the Federation's Economics Department. My job mainly entailed trying to stop merchants importing more chickens, pigs and turkeys from South Africa or the Belgian Congo, in order to protect local farmers, than my boss deemed necessary. Fortunately for me I had a pleasant motherly secretary who handled the irate applicants. Looking back, having worked in very many countries since then I can only marvel at an administrative system which dispensed valuable permits without having to worry about bribery.

My responsibilities, with such an admirable secretary to do all the work, were not demanding and entailed an increase in salary and allowed me to visit some of the remoter part of the Colony which included the Victoria Falls. It also enabled me to get to know, through working and social contacts, staff of the Colonial Service, an organisation that had foolishly rejected my recruitment as being too dangerous for them. Last, but not least, the high quality hostel in which I resided was next door to the Nurses, Home, which was inhabited by attractive young nurses.

But first the Colonial system. I always felt a little like Alice going through the looking glass as I crossed the Zambezi River into Northern Rhodesia from the south. The 350 mile journey, from the capital of Southern Rhodesia to Lusaka the capital of Northern Rhodesia, even entailed a 50 mile break as the road dropped down into the hot steamy Zambezi Valley before rising again to the Lusaka Plateau. Southern Rhodesia was a bustling dynamic European working- class society with few obvious social distinctions between Europeans. Northern Rhodesia, on the other hand, apart from the northern Copper belt, was a more languorous, laid-back, liberal society ruled by rather superior sorts of people from Oxbridge who were remote from commerce, or indeed development, and to whom protocol played a rather higher role in social life than it did in the South.

Apart from the three small prosperous copper mine towns in the north, almost wholly European, and a few European farmers scraping a living along the "line of rail", it still seemed much of a subsistence economy. Lusaka, the capital, was a one-road town surrounded by large passionately red-flowering spathodia trees in the neat European suburbs with a distant African township. The Governor pranced around in a cocked hat and Provincial Commissioners drove around with Union Jacks on their cars.

On one occasion a nervous Secretary for Agriculture asked me to fly out to Fort Jameson with him, a three hour flight in a shaky Dakota, to confront what he expected to be aggressive European farmers who through age and remoteness could no longer make a living from farming. He assumed that my professional skills might be used like a wand to dissipate their anger at being neglected by the Government. We were met at the dusty airport by his chum the Provincial Commissioner, a stout character in a tweed jacket with a loud cheery voice – "wood all through" a colleague had warned me before I left – who regaled my anxious colleague for an hour on the latest Test Cricket results (it may have been a Compton period), as his large flag-flying automobile swept through primitive African villages. We returned later in the day having never met the angry farmers.

I had to admit, however, the Colonial administrators were an entertaining lot and did have the welfare of the subjects uppermost in their minds. They also provided as honest an administration as a country is ever likely to get. Indeed as I went on to work in non-colonies such as Ethiopia, where they openly lamented that they had never been colonised, to Latin America where the efficient honest public administrator was the exception rather than the rule, I came to appreciate their qualities of integrity and efficiency. These qualities are very rare and almost totally absent in most developing countries. I often longed to have someone of the competence and integrity of the average Colonial Administrator in the many Governments in Latin America with whom I later worked, upon whom I could rely.

Both in Northern Rhodesia, and Nyasaland which I got to know later, the Colonial Administration provided a system of Government which I am sure many Africans, as they survey the shattered societies in which so many now have to live, must look back upon nostalgically as a golden era of stability and justice.

SOCIAL LIFE

While there was plenty of interesting work to keep any reasonably energetic young man busy in Southern Rhodesia , social life was not exactly stimulating. Indeed, apart from the occasional tennis match, a good amateur theatre and a very good modern art gallery, it was distinctly dull. Very masculine oriented and alcohol oriented.

And it was entirely European. There were very few Africans educated beyond secondary school and none served in the public administration in anything but extremely junior levels. In Salisbury there was only one location where Europeans and Africans could mix socially and this was a club established by liberal Europeans, which Africans could join. It was, however, very small.

Lusaka opened up a distinctly more promising social life. Although I was at a distinct social disadvantage coming from the new brash Federal Service, instead of the Oxbridge Colonial Service, any new face was always welcome and treated hospitably. As mentioned earlier, in the adjoining European Nurses Home there was a goodly supply of sprightly nurses who brightened one's social life.

One day hearing the lively sounds of tennis matches in the grounds of the nurses mess next door I strolled over with the thought that this offered an opportunity for some exercise. There was a mixed doubles taking place. One of the female players was the focus of many male eyes as they pretended to be interested in the tennis. Dressed in the briefest of shorts which showed off her elegant legs at their best and with neat short- sleeved blouse, near perfect features and large brown eyes, she was by far the most attractive girl I had seen. The fact that her tennis skills were minimal and she waved her tennis racket around wildly when the ball did not come anywhere near did not seem to worry the spectators at all. Her helpless distress at the failure of the ball to come close enough to enable her return it in fact aroused their sympathies. Her male partner was red with exhaustion attempting to cover the court.

I immediately thought that I needed to get to know this girl. It was clear that there were many, very many, who had the same idea. Discreet enquiries revealed she was a nurse called Jean, from Teignmouth in Devon, where it was reported she had been a "Miss Teignmouth 1948" and who had been working in the Federation for six years and unbelievably was single and unattached. Well more or less, as there were many suitors, the Governor's aide de camp, doctors, District Commissioners, policemen, indeed any unattached male seemed to be interested. She was even part of the Governor's entourage. What chance had a parvenu from the distinctly social down- market Southern Rhodesia have here? Not much.

Her entourage, which I joined, drifted over for tea at the nurses home, where she charmingly told us how disappointed she was that her roses had refused to bloom despite fertilizing them with human blood surpluses from the hospital. While her admirers shared her distress and I would not have been surprised had several offered fresh blood, I decided that such a servile response was not what any real woman would want. In fact I protested strongly at the use of what could well have been my blood for this purpose. She seemed a little surprised by my response. My competitors turned on me with surprise that I had expressed such unchivalrous sentiments and assured her that they all supported her.

Noticing that she seemed a little chastened by my comments I crept back to the rose garden that evening and attached the plentiful bougainvillea flowers which grew there to her rose bushes. Although I left no "signature" I felt sure she would be touched by my concern.

Then I had a stroke of luck. Maybe it was not luck – just that good fortune favours those who look for it. My Secretary in Lusaka had a husband who was Chairman of the local Lusaka Film Club. And he, or they, wished to produce a tourist film about Lusaka. Anything as desperate or crazy as a film seeking to attract visitors to a capital which had one road with lots of scruffy Asian shops and one modern building is difficult to imagine. It is true the main road was exotically called "Cairo Road", named by that heroic pioneer Cecil Rhodes, as a commitment to build a railway to from Cape Town to Cairo, but apart from photographing the nameplate it is difficult to think how it could become a tourist attraction.

However, all this was beside the point. I was asked if I would take the lead part as a visiting tourist. The only time I had been on the stage was as the hind part of the donkey in a pantomime in Buenos Aires and I had dragged my brother, who was the front part, down on top of me, as I failed to sit on a waiting chair. The sight of a flailing front legs collapsing over its back legs brought the house down and ensured the pantomime's success and was the main talking point of the theatrical world in Buenos Aires for a long time. However, I decided not to reveal this distinctly dodgy thespian past and accepted the part graciously. And who should be my leading lady but this cynosure of all male eyes. I could not believe my luck.

We were photographed as she showed me all the delights of Lusaka and I was allowed to give her a chaste farewell kiss as I left this African tourist Eden forever. Unfortunately my acting skills were not all that great. I was told to look at her as if I were in love with her. Unfortunately my eye balls and the rest of my face did not seem to coordinate very well and many repeat shots had to be taken. In exasperation the producer said "Imagine she is an Argentine steak." This did not please her at all but it at last seemed to please the producer.

Fortunately she did not take offence and was intrigued by my Argentine connection as her father had visited "romantic" Buenos Aires where "Tangos were danced in the streets." I did not disillusion her. I could not dance the tango and no one danced tangos in the streets – they would get run over. In fact very few Argentines danced the tango.

She was fortunately tolerant of my acting weaknesses and patient with me, not too critical and to use a metaphor, at least I had "a foot in the door".

I could not believe my luck when some weeks later, I daringly suggested to her that we might spend a week at a holiday resort off the Mozambique coast suitably called Paradise Island and she agreed. She did not tell me till later she was bringing a friend. Oh well-dreams!

While I was waiting for her to drive down from Lusaka to embark on this dreamy holiday, the telephone rang to say that there had been a car accident in the Zambezi Valley and she was in hospital in Lusaka with a broken arm and leg. It appeared that her friend who was driving had gone into a skid and in a panic had turned the car over.

She was quite surprised and impressed to find me at her bedside, which was full of flowers from rivals and bottles of champagne the following day, having driven the 350 miles in a mere seven hours. She was recovering well; her driver friend being thrown clear was unhurt. Since she took a few weeks to recover I found that I could visit her over the week-end by leaving Salisbury very early on Saturday morning and arriving at about 2 pm seven hours later. I had a day before returning on Sunday afternoon. The relationship was coming on quite well.

It may well have been this assiduous interest, plus the nonchalant confidence with which I then claimed that I was planning to become Prime Minister which later triggered a favourable response to my suggestion that our relationship would benefit if it were made permanent. Power, or even the claim to it, as I learned later, is the most strongest of aphrodisiacs. Whatever it was, my social and personal life changed forever, as she agreed to my proposal.

We organised our own wedding, no relatives being remotely near, in Salisbury and settled comfortably in a romantic rondavel in a huge colourful garden and with our own houseboy. The rondavel consisted of two round shaped rooms separated by a covered thatched patio off which there was bathroom and a kitchen. It had no security of any sort, no doors would lock. In those days Africa was a very safe place.

Our social life flourished, as there were many young white couples like us who provided lively companionship. Our only contact with the African population was through our servants.

This appalling barrier was one which Jean, and other liberal friends not tied to the Civil Service, challenged by organising a joint protest movement with blacks, and seeking entrance to the shops, hotels, bars and cinema facilities. This was not always well received by the less well-educated, less liberal white population. I recall one occasion when it was proposed that African Professional Civil Servants should be allowed to join the Professional Association which had been set up to promote our interests but this was rejected by a small majority at a well-attended public meeting.

Indeed it is easy to be liberal about African advancement if one's job is unlikely to be challenged, and the majority of Whites in Southern Rhodesia saw in African advancement a challenge to their job skills. And they were right.

But in the establishment of the Federation this social reality was brushed aside by the hope that economic growth and white long-term interests would overcome racial prejudice and eventually accept a multi-racial society dominated by Africans.

We lived this dream for a while. We produced a new male citizen, Jeremy, for the Federation and purchased an acre of bush where we would go and picnic and dream of a house where we would live in domestic bliss in a liberal new society.

Alas this dream was not to be. Africa was cracking. The adjoining Belgian Congo which had enriched Belgium for decades with its wealth of copper was suddenly granted independence, but the burning long- suppressed resentment at years of ill- treatment led the native inhabitants taking over these splendid assets to embark on an orgy of looting and rape which had Belgians running for their lives into Northern Rhodesia, and the United Nations having to send in troops to restore some semblance of order.

While we made the comfortable assumption that such events would not occur in the wiser liberal run colonies of Northern Rhodesia and Nyasaland, and might be contained in Southern Rhodesia, (if the Whites were sufficiently sensible to adapt to demographic reality), it was never realistic to expect that life would be quite the same in this European dominated Federation. The subsequent burning to death of an unfortunate European woman, in liberal Northern Rhodesia of all places, by an African crowd, brought it home to us that if we wanted a safer and happier future it was unlikely to be in central Africa.

So, after eight years of Jean's life in Africa and four years of my own, we were fortunate enough, to secure a job with the United Nations in Ethiopia, and with many regrets left what should be, could be, an arcadia. However, a generous and beautiful environment is no guarantee of peace. And so it was – not.

LOOKING BACK

It was nearly fifteen years later, after working in Ethiopia and Latin America, and returning to Britain when the Labour Government set up a Ministry of Overseas Development, that my early career in Africa impinged upon my current one. One of my responsibilities was to advise the Government on its aid programmes in Africa and these three ex- colonies fell within my brief.

In the intervening period the Federation had been abolished, Northern Rhodesia had been granted independence and had become Zambia and Nyasaland had become Malawi. The whites, in Southern Rhodesia, made a Unilateral Declaration of Independence from Britain in 1965, which led to universal international condemnation, other than from the white government in neighbouring South Africa. Unfortunately for the Whites this move was not popular with Africans and they had started a guerrilla war which increased to such effect over a period of years that the tiny white population realised they could not go on.

Various failed negotiations took place, the Foreign Office, our parent body, being responsible. Although we in the Development Administration played no part in them, nor were we asked our advice, I volunteered a solution to the apparent problem of so much land being in the hands of a sector of the population whose agricultural output played a key role in the economy.

I sent a memo to my Under Secretary suggesting that he propose to the Foreign Office negotiators a policy for any new African Government by which a) they nationalised all land in Southern Rhodesia b) gave long- term leases to all European farmers of say 15/20 years and c) guaranteed farmers that at the end of that period they could take a certain amount of foreign exchange if they wished to leave the country.

To my mind this brilliant idea allowed the Government a political policy triumph but accepted economic reality that European farmers were vital to the economy and could not be adequately replaced for many years.

I was told that my suggestion had reached "dizzy heights" and was called to a meeting with a team of US negotiators under the peripatetic leadership of the great Henry Kissinger who had been roped in to use his supposed diplomatic skills to sort out this problem. They listened to my proposal with some scepticism, not having come across the concept of leasehold ownership in the USA but it was accepted that this idea was part of the package being proposed.

I was never told what if anything became of these negotiations though I heard that they never discussed the issue of land ownership.

It was another couple of years before an independence agreement was hammered out, in 1980, which dealt with the vital land issue, in what I thought was a most unrealistic fashion. It was that the new Government would gradually buy out European land "at market prices", with funds provided by the British Government. It seemed ridiculous to me that it was possible to determine "market price" if one was dealing with 42 % of the country, as well as being pretty unfair that the new Government had to buy back its own country, admittedly with British Aid money. And secondly that there simply would not be enough funds to achieve this.

Nevertheless, the new Zimbabwe accepted this proposal. The leadership appreciated that they were taking over what the new President of neighbouring Mozambique called the "jewel of Africa".

I had the good fortune to visit the country two years after independence in 1982, and was no end surprised to find the European way of life little affected. I was expecting great African resentment towards Europeans after the very nasty civil war. Far from it. It was one of the friendliest countries of the many I had since visited that I had come across, despite the many years of injustice which so many Africans experienced.

I paid a visit to Parliament where I was astonished to find on the opposition bench Ian Smith, the defeated white Prime Minister who must bear the blame for so much of the disaster of the civil war, in a debate about internment, and objecting to the fact that an MP had been illegally interned and tortured. Government MPs jeered him and pointed out that he had introduced these internment laws, though his counter argument was that since they were no longer at war these laws were no longer justified. It was cheering and surprising to encounter this vigorous debate though the intervention of one African MP, who stated of the MP "he is an old man and should be killed," made one suspect that the concepts of democracy and justice had some way to go.

Nevertheless, the Government was careful for nearly another two decades not to kill the Golden Goose. On reflection outsiders had not appreciated that agricultural land, not even 42 % of it, was not a political or social problem. The newly educated African elite did not want to run farms. They were interested in jobs in urban areas in the public administration, in business, in politics and in the armed services. This is where the real rewards lay, not in working and living in remote rural areas.

But meanwhile, mismanagement and corruption gradually enveloped this new country. There was no way the President was going to give up power regardless of election results. And this is when, around 2001, the European farmers made their fatal mistake. They sided with, and openly supported financially, the opposition. The Government reacted with viciousness and speed by encouraging invasion and takeover of European farms regardless of the devastating economic effects of seizing these high- value farms. The Government gave most of them to favourites who could no more run a farm or wished to, than they could fly an aeroplane. Several white farmers were killed in the process. Hell hath no fury than a despot whose power is challenged. The fact that tens of thousands of African employees were made destitute, that exports collapsed, that inflation took on four- figure digits, that most of the population were no longer supporting him, was of no consequence.

As Lord Acton said "All power tends to corrupt and absolute power corrupts absolutely."

It was the end of the last remnants of a "white" Africa – the beginning of a black one.

Chapter Three

AN AFRICAN EMPIRE

The letter was from New York in an attractive blue and red lined envelope from the United Nations office. Dated 16 August 1960 it started "Dear Sir", The Secretary General of the United Nations directs me to inform you that your application for a post at the UN Economic Commission for Africa in Ethiopia has been accepted". It went on to establish my grade and details of appointment and asked me to confirm my acceptance.

I was most impressed that the Secretary General should have taken the trouble to write to me, though on reading it I was disappointed to find Dag Hammerskjold's signature was not at the bottom of the letter. Maybe he had more important matters to attend to.

Never mind. It was the content which counted. A job, a permanent one, with the United Nations.

Was this not my original youthful aspiration and that of many public-spirited internationally oriented youths, to serve, to save, the world? But one very few were ever likely to realize as it was not just noble aspirations or qualifications or even experience, which counted, but one's nationality. United Nations posts were allocated by quota to Member nation nationals depending upon their contribution to the budget. The British quota was always over- full.

But here luck was on my side. I had an Argentine passport, as well as a British one – and there were not all that many Argentines with two economics degrees from respectable British Universities and with four years experience in Africa. So I had, with an admirable appreciation of my international loyalties, applied as an Argentine citizen.

The offer could not have been better timed. Although having a very satisfying job in central Africa, the future for whites in that part of the world was starting to look distinctly dodgy And although I had come to have some professional doubts about joining what might be a huge international bureaucracy, these were soon dissipated when I realised that UN salaries, which were based on those in the USA, would treble our income, and as a bonus I would get home leave once every two years to Buenos Aires, with my family, first class into the bargain. This was too good to be true.

No way could I refuse this generous offer. So soon we bade a sad farewell to many lively young friends and were headed for Ethiopia.

ETHIOPIA

This remote highland country, which for centuries had created its own unique culture, had been the object of mystery and legend to Europeans over the ages.

It was the land of Pester John, of the legendary Queen of Sheba, the home of one of the lost tribes of Israel and a remote island of Coptic Christianity in a sea of Islam and paganism. It was claimed that the ancient Kingdom of Kaffiria in southern Ethiopia was the origin of coffee.

Early medieval European pioneers reported with disbelief the huge rock churches of Lalibela, and the first British book by James Bruce on his three years in the highlands in the 1770s, in which he reported on the customs of the people, were greeted with incredulity; a people who ate raw meat sliced off live cattle, one of his more unattractive claims, was disbelieved.

In the nineteenth century however, European encroachment in Africa was starting to make itself felt. In 1867 some 5,000 British and Indian troops, complete with Indian elephants, trailed up from the coast to rescue the British Consul and some missionaries who the Emperor Theodore had unwisely imprisoned. The objective was accomplished with little bloodshed, though at considerable financial cost for those days of £ 9m, but no attempt was made to establish a foothold in the country, as Disraeli and the Government wanted no more financial entanglements in Africa. General Napier, the leader of this mighty expedition, earned himself a place in history as one of the now lesser-known sculptures on a plinth in Trafalgar Square.

In 1878, at the Congress of Berlin, where larger European countries carved up Africa between them, Italy was left out. Stung by this Italy decided to take a slice of Abyssinia and from a base in Massawa on the coast attacked Emperor Menelik with some 9,000 Italian and Colonial troops only to suffer the greatest defeat a European power ever experienced in Africa.

An important factor in this defeat was the supply of rifles which the French, anxious to establish a link between their Red Sea base in Djibouti, had provided to Emperor Menelik to allow them to link up with their colonies in West Africa. Menelik was also able to use this huge increase in firepower to extend his rule southwards by exterminating and enslaving the Galla tribes of the south and establishing the frontiers of modern Ethiopia.

Meanwhile a young, 32-year-old, intrepid Frenchman Le Marchand, was making his laborious way over the 750 miles of forest, desert and swamp, to link up with the French Ethiopian team on the Nile. He eventually reached a deserted island at Fashoda to find that Menelik's deviousness had ensured that his French counterpart had missed him, and whom should he meet instead but General Kitchener who with his 25,000- man army had just decimated the Mahdi army with highly efficient machine guns, and avenged Gordon's death, at Omdurman. The race to the middle of nowhere, a struggle for a totally useless link between north and south or east and west created "The Fashoda Crisis" and nearly led to war between Britain and France. However, the French blinked first and what became known as the Sudan was absorbed into British- ruled Egypt.

Back in Ethiopia, Menelik and the dominant Amharas established themselves as the ruling aristocracy. And a very superior people they were. Slavery continued right into the 1920's and 1930's when that intrepid woman traveller Rosita Forbes recounts meeting slave columns from the south on their way to the "eunuch factories" at Harar in the North, and then on to the Arab societies of the Gulf.

In 1935 the Italians, anxious for a place "in the African sun", once more attacked Ethiopia and this time outgunned the defenders. The Emperor Haile Selassie had to flee making an impassioned plea for help before the League of Nations which was ignored. He sought exile, a small dignified figure, in Bath.

Finally the Italian declaration of war on the Allied powers led to a British invasion from Kenya and the Sudan in 1940 which resulted in the very rapid defeat of the Italians in Ethiopia and the return of the Emperor to a freed country.

The African Empire was back.

However, European military incursions were not the only events which brought this country to European or British attention. For those of a literary inclination, Ethiopia appears on the world stage as Azania in Evelyn Waugh's two great social and political satires," Black Mischief" and " Scoop". Who can forget his opening to the former "We, Seth, Emperor of Azania, Chief of Sakuyu, Lord of Wanda and Tyrant of the Seas, Bachelor of Arts of Oxford University"? This hilarious satire leaves us with an indelible account of a society and characters caught between the medieval world and the modern.

Having read both books before leaving for this mysterious exotic African Empire, we thought that these no doubt exaggerated satires would over two decades or more have faded with time and real life would bear little resemblance to Waugh's accounts of it.

We were not entirely right.

ARRIVAL

In those days flying was not like entering a huge overcrowded cinema but entailed excitement and a sense of danger. One was never quite sure for, example, whether the propellers which revolved with deafening noise just outside one's window had been securely attached by ground crew and one wondered what would happen if one propeller came off. To add to the excitement, flames would occasionally shoot out of the rear of the engines but would disappear just as one was about to consult the air hostess about this alarming phenomenon. And just as one had accustomed oneself to the steady roar of the engines they would, alarmingly suddenly, alter their rhythm for no obvious reason and one cast furtive glances out of the window to ensure they were still there - perhaps one of them had come loose? .

Neither did they fly very high, though this had the advantage that we could see, after take-off from Nairobi as we flew over bleak, yellow lands, the Masai tribesmen, famous for their ferociousness and diet of cattle urine, cattle blood and milk, herding their cattle. It also meant that the hot African afternoon sun created currents which tossed aircraft around in an alarming way.

But suddenly the tiny human dots in the desert below disappeared and we were skimming over forests and mountains. This was not because the pilot had altered his height but we were now over the Ethiopian highlands which were 8,500 feet high. Hoping that the pilot had a good view of any obstructions in his flight path, we were able to have a splendid view over southern Ethiopia.

"Wow," cried Jean with excitement "it's just like Switzerland." She was right though in this case there were no snow-covered mountains, but the varied mountainous landscapes with blazing green valleys and raging rivers, were a vision of colourful surprise. The comparison with Switzerland was surprising but fair.

Our subsequent travels around the central plateau of the Ethiopian highlands confirmed the splendid lush green beauty of this mountain island. Admittedly the recent rains, which led to glistening green pastures and the wild flowering of beautiful yellow "Maskel" daises, heightened our first impressions. Later, as we travelled north and south of Addis Ababa, we found, not the sparse starving badlands which become so familiar on television in later years, but a country of green valleys, lakes, blue hills, rushing streams and tall eucalyptus trees. Indeed an early British traveller (Major Henry Darley, author of "Slaves and Ivory in Abyssinia") wrote "Some of our camping grounds on the verge of pleasant water meadows backed by charming little copses made it almost impossible to believe that we were really in Africa and we spent much of our time laying out in our imagination the estates on which we would like to spend our old age." Major Darley goes on to say "Kaffa is really the loveliest country I have ever seen – mostly forest country, with open glades and running streams, reminding one of England in summer time."

The "badlands" were to the north where steep, denuded, mountain slopes fed soil to the Sudanese and Egyptians and left little fertility to those struggling on their tiny terraces.

The pilot eventually navigated us successfully over the coffee forests, over occasional hills and bounced onto Addis Ababa airstrip.

Accustomed as we had been to the "Europeanised" Africa we were in for a shock. The terminal was packed with masses of Ethiopians who were anxious either to board flights or greet arrivals, and guards with long canes would set about them when they became unruly, seeking to control them.

And they were dressed quite differently the women in distinctive shawls and skirts of fine white cotton and for men in white leggings or jodhpurs, quite different from the rest of black Africa where European clothing was the norm. When clean this dress was very impressive and especially when decorated with elaborate coloured borders, very fetching, but unless washed or changed frequently it became drably discoloured. Poverty meant that what could be a beautiful dress became shabby.

The vast majority of Ethiopians had fine firm features, held themselves erect and the women had long black hair. They were a handsome race. As we were driven from the airport we were struck by the differences from Europeanised East, Southern and Central Africa.

The pot holed road was crowded with undisciplined traffic in the form of tiny battered blue Italian taxis, "garys" which were two-wheeled taxi carts pulled by small semi starved horses, energetically encouraged by whip- waving drivers, by confused flocks of sheep and occasionally cattle. From time to time very superior- looking men, in pith helmets and flowing white "shammas" elegantly dressed on horseback would canter past with a retainer running behind.

The houses on the roadside were normally mud huts with thatched roofs but dismal practical, corrugated- iron ones were rapidly replacing them. Along some stretches of road corrugated iron sheeting had been put up by the Government to hide from visiting dignitaries the embarrassing sight of urban poverty.

Addis Ababa itself was founded only at the beginning of the twentieth century when the imported Australian eucalyptus trees produced such quick growing sources of firewood that the Imperial Court's fuel needs could be met, and was able to settle on one site. Indeed, set in a green fertile valley surrounded by hills and the ubiquitous eucalyptus ,it was a beautiful location. Alas the general poverty of the country meant that it was a town of shacks, with a sprinkling of modern buildings around the town square built mainly in Italian times.

The drive up to the town centre, along Churchill Avenue, was lined by small single- storey corrugated- iron- roofed buildings of artisan traders and shops. One stood out vividly with a huge advertisement "Coffins, coffins, and coffins". Many others had little purple or green crosses outside of them. These were brothels. In an article Time magazine delicately explained that customers seeking medical help who came "for treatment, got treats" The colours indicated whether drinks were provided as well.

For those knowledgeable of India it was very similar to a small bustling poverty- stricken provincial town. True there were some signs of the modern world in the Italian building legacy, dull solid classic architecture, a large modern hotel and a block of luxury flats. In addition the recently completed massive six-storey new home of the United Nations Economic Commission for African stood, with a splendid façade and imposing entrance, as a hope for a new Africa.

The poverty was a paradox. How could this beautiful fertile landscape not have at least led to a comfortable Shangri –La? There were two reasons. One was its isolation from the rest of the world and the huge transport costs of exporting any of its agricultural products. The railway, a tortuous and poorly run system of communication, dated from the turn of the century, and the first decent motor road to the coast had been only been built by the Italians in the late 1930s.

The only exports of significance, which could bear these transport costs, were slaves, coffee and ivory .Although the former trade was supposed to have declined or disappeared in the 1930s, as Ethiopia promised to ban it when joining the League of Nations, it still continued but in a hidden fashion as until there emerged a more thriving economy which could afford wage labour, slavery could not be eliminated.

Wild coffee of high quality was produced in the fertile forests of the south but distance, poor roads and the wild coffee trees (which are not easy to pick) were significant disadvantages despite very low labour costs which probably included some form of slave labour.

The second main reason was social and political. Land was parcelled out to Governors known as "Rases", feudal overlords, upon whom the Emperor was heavily dependent for his position and who held total power over their people. Since none of the Governors was paid they had to live off "the land" and the main easy source of income was the sale of slaves. Governors whose appointments were likely to be transient would carry off as many slaves as possible when transferred, leaving a decimated population and economy. The incoming Governor then had to raid adjoining areas for slaves to "survive". The whole of the south during the first half of the nineteenth[h] and for several decades into the twentieth century was ravaged and decimated by ruthless Amharic "overlords".

Ironically, the only independent country in Africa was the one where slavery was widely practised.

Had peasant ownership been been established, a small enterprising reasonably prosperous class could have emerged. In fact there were some Ras and Governors who were wise, and able to offer stability and sensible levels of taxation, and under these all too rare circumstance peasants prospered.

This geographical isolation, this remoteness, combined with a still semi -feudal society, made this a quite unique but impoverished African Empire. It provided us with endless surprises, many new friends and an insight to a society not all that different from that visited by Evelyn Waugh twenty five years earlier.

A SUPERIOR PEOPLE

The Amharas, who had been the ruling group in Ethiopia for at least a century and half were an impressively self-confident people. Emperor Haile Selassie, who had reigned since 1923, even claimed that he was descended from Solomon and Sheba. He was a "Lion of Judah" and kept tame lions in his palace.

It was refreshing, having come from colonial societies to encounter this self-confidence, although one felt sometimes that it was carried a bit far. Certainly their views on other tribes and countries bore comparison with the views of many white Rhodesian farmers.

The Ethiopians we met and befriended were all university- trained, in Britain or the USA, and were as entertaining and lively a group of people we were likely to meet anywhere. We were very surprised when on several occasions we were told: "Oh Gordon. You do not understand. We never had the advantages of British rule as the Ghanaians and Nigerians had." This was very confusing. Had I not believed that one of my functions was to relieve Africans of colonial rule?

Imperial rule in Ethiopia, if it is not a contradiction, was liberal and reformist and the Emperor had been gradually seeking to drag the country into the twentieth century. He carried himself with severe dignity and there was every sign that he was well respected. However, the custom of the local inhabitants prostrating themselves on the pavements as his entourage swept past did seem a trifle medieval. Europeans were excused such a demanding athletic performance and we were only asked to stop our cars get out and bow. Jean, a great stickler for royal etiquette, nearly brained herself on the car roof as she too hastily leapt out of the car to bow to HIM.

The Emperor's power depended on the control which his regional Ras' held over the population. Although there was a powerful army and a feeble police force that half-heartedly sought bribes, he had an elite personal guard, the Imperial Guard, upon whom he showered education and glittering uniforms. They were his guarantee of safety.

It was not from our point of view an oppressive regime, though guns, admittedly very ancient ones, were the normal feature of life. On one occasion at a Committee meeting at a Government office, a middle-rank Ethiopian, while tidying out his pocket, put his revolver on the table. This went unremarked by anyone at the meeting. However, this proliferation made one feel a little uneasy about rural travel for in the Africa we had lived in guns were virtually unknown and theft and assaults on rural travellers unheard of. Not that one was in any real danger in Ethiopia, it just looked as if it could be dangerous if things got out of hand. However a perceptive Major Darley wrote in 1935: "Should any of the subject races obtain rifles and ammunition in any quantity a civil war is a certainty with all its massacres and extermination."

Access to the Emperor on public occasions was disarmingly easy if one was a European and had a camera. One of the first religious festivals we attended was that of Timcat – to celebrate the end of the rains. A huge timber, pyramid bonfire brilliantly decorated with bright yellow flowers, was prepared on a traffic island. Around it were gathered as colourful a collection of priests as one is likely to encounter anywhere. They were dressed in gorgeous white cloaks, or beautiful bright red cloaks all embroidered with silver and gold threads, carrying even more gaily embroidered parasols of rich ornate, velvet materials in green, yellow and red. We were pushed almost against our will through the massive crowds and a policeman even escorted us to the very front where we were only a few yards from HIM as he appeared in a shiny Rolls Royce. After much chanting and parading the pyramid was lit and burst into flames amongst cheers from the crowds.

On another colourful occasion we witnessed the celebrations to welcome back Ato Abebe Bikila who had just become the country's first Olympic gold medallist having run 26 kilometres without stopping – something he used to do delivering the post at 8,500 feet. There was a huge parade with about 2000 khaki clad soldiers not marching in unison but all shuffling, gyrating and dancing yet being able to do this in reasonable order as like a gigantic brown snail they moved down the road. They were followed by some 50 Galla horsemen on brilliant white steeds, wearing lion-mane headdresses, dressed in white with green and red sashes and carrying lances and gold- gilded circular purple and red shields- as impressive a medieval scene as one is likely to see outside a film set. They were followed by the modern world of 30 gleaming chromium motorcycle cops on chromium bikes. And then to remind us that we were in Ethiopia a lethargic old lion sitting on the bonnet of a jeep with the co-driver holding on to his tail. Finally the hero of the day waving on a huge truck followed by a cavalcade of cars, many of which kept breaking down.

Evelyn Waugh would have loved it.

LIVING

We moved into a three -bedroomed house built some 30 years earlier during the Italian days – solid adobe with a corrugated iron roof, it stood in about half an acre of garden with precarious fence of wooden staves and a huge metal gate. There were no "European" areas in Addis Ababa, so with few exceptions one found oneself in a social island surrounded by smoky mud huts and tall eucalyptus trees. Actually there were a few areas where a clutch of European-style houses was being provided for the ever-increasing inflow of overpaid foreign experts and UN bureaucrats. But these were dull and built too close together for comfort.

Our house was just off the main road and was nearly opposite what appeared to be a derelict factory site but it turned out to be the army barracks. A safe location, as Jean was to discover later, it was not. We would often encounter evil-looking hyenas lurking outside our garden gate when we drove home at night.

In order to maintain our establishment we firstly had to employ a guard to protect us from bandits and burglars. Mandivoro, the first and successful applicant offered to do both the twelve- hour shifts if we paid him for one and a half shifts. This seemed a good financial deal to me, so he was employed. His role was hardly a demanding one as his only job was to open the gate twice a day to let the car through and to cut the grass occasionally.

The only burglar we ever had was, ironically, one who broke into Mandivoro's room when he was asleep, neglecting his 24 hour responsibility, and stole a couple of his shirts. My softhearted wife insisted that these be replaced by some of my own, something which seemed to me a rather strange way of rewarding failure.

However, he did excel himself on a later occasion.

Then we had to employ Said, a tall handsome male who claimed he could cook, and a nursemaid, Yeshie, to look after our only child. Since she had a child herself she employed a young girl to look after her child. All in all we had six people living in the servant's quarters.

At least part of my inflated United Nations salary was being put to good employment use.

Mandivoro's day of heroism occurred this way. The servants had their own cesspit loo at the bottom of the garden. It consisted of a tiny shed with an eight foot- pit and a box with a hole in it. One day we heard screams. Our nanny's nanny had taken the baby she was looking after to the loo and accidentally dropped her down this appalling hell hole. What a to do? What was I expected to do? Fortunately the gallant Mandivoro was to hand and with a rope held by others he lowered himself into the mess and hauled out the baby. What a hero! This time I did not begrudge him the shirt Jean gave him.

The countryside produced a wide range of fruit and vegetables which could be purchased at the market, but every item, from lettuces to potatoes, required at least five minutes of bargaining. Meat was not a problem if one was not too fussy. The butcher had his shop in a sort of portable garden shed at the top of the road. There was a single window which was the serving hatch and as one peered in one saw masses of hunks of meat hanging from the ceiling with the butcher dodging between them. They were large solid chunks of meat, which were quite unrecognisable – other than filet. One paid about a £1 for a complete fillet so this was what we usually bought. We were a bit taken aback to discover that the butcher slept in this wooden charnel house and were quite relieved and surprised to find one day that he had up- shed and moved away.

Our milk used to come in an assortment of wine or whisky bottles. Since corks were in short supply they were stopped up with the plentiful eucalyptus leaves which gave the milk a quite exotic taste, even though we always boiled it.

We were occasionally tempted to try Ethiopian food at restaurants specially opened to attract us "feranji". The main dish was spicy meat served on a sour, grey spongy pancake, which tasted a bit like a dry mattress. It was not as bad as it sounds, but not a dish which one would wish to depend upon.

It was left to Jean to seek to master Amharic, for without some form of verbal exchange with our servants life was going to be tricky, so within a few weeks she was able to muster the basic words she needed to survive.

Social life was quite a revelation, as the United Nations comprised every conceivable nationality and we all mixed together very well without any social or cultural problems. Despite very different backgrounds, we all had a common professional liberality and there were no national or racial hang-ups. We found the Egyptians to be the most hospitable and extremely entertaining.

After a while, however, we found the lack of entertainment rather limiting so it occurred to me it would be a good idea to form a film society. My experience in this area was somewhat limited but when living in Hampstead I had seen lots of film society fare such as " Battleship Potemkin", " Jour de Fete", and it seemed to me such similar enlightenment might be well received in Addis Ababa.

The United Nations Personnel Officer agreed that I could use the huge United Nations auditorium and its projector to show the films. The problem was how could I get a regular supply of films? The only source I discovered was South Africa and they would provide them but how to get them to Ethiopia? Solution? The British Embassy. Their First Secretary was a splendidly helpful chap with an interest in films and he agreed to the Diplomatic Bag being used for this valuable purpose.

My problem was that I really did not know much about Classic Films. My first choice was "An Italian Straw Hat". Much to my amazement 300 people turned up for the showing – it was free mind you – and applause broke out at the end of a charming Embassy.

The next, whose name now escapes me, was equally successful. But the third whose name is etched painfully in my memory was called "Nanook of the North". I had heard it was a famous documentary and I vaguely hopefully equated it to that famous rude song "Eskimo Nell.

An eager audience awaited its presentation. It was an old film - a very old film – about 1925 and it was about Eskimos in the arctic. But it had become famous as it recorded Eskimos pulling seals out of holes in the ice. A tug of war broke out. Sometimes the hidden seal pulled skidding Eskimos towards the hole, and then with superhuman effort they regained their strength and moved away from it. This went on for about five minutes and one wondered what was going to come next. Had the seals got together to form a team? The audience was becoming restless. After 10 minutes without resolution one or two started to leave. After 20 minutes with this desperate struggle still undecided most of the audience had left and after half an hour of this dramatically undecided challenge only the organiser and his wife were left. We switched off without knowing who the victors were. So ended the brief life of the Addis Ababa Film Society.

WORKING

The whole purpose of this exciting move to Ethiopia was of course to work for the United Nations - what more noble a task than international public service? I therefore awaited the meeting with my new boss, Adrian, with great interest.

He was a handsome middle-aged Australian and was Head of the UN/FAO Agricultural Unit which I joined as a junior member.

His greeting was cheerful but not a little disconcerting "What's a bright young chap like you doing joining this golden cage?" Ignoring the unmerited compliment I thought he might have been a little more positive. Sure I was aware of the golden glitter attached to my new role but the metaphor of cage took me aback. I was going to free the world from poverty and oppression via the United Nations.

He explained that most of our work entailed "servicing" United Nations Committees with reports on the agricultural and economic situation in Africa and that there could be occasional technical assistance to individual countries.

Within a few days I realised that writing annual reports, which I correctly anticipated were unlikely to be read, let alone be implemented, was not a life for which six hard years of university life had trained me, and I would not find it very satisfying.

This early sense of frustration was not one which many of my amiable colleagues shared. One was a very pleasant Egyptian with a beautiful wife half his age, who had been kicked out of Egypt as he had warned his superiors that the Aswan Dam would be a disaster as alluvium was substituted for artificial fertiliser and would eventually silt up the dam.

Another was a fat jolly Liberian, with eight children whose transport and education costs would have bankrupted any commercial organisation, who only stayed a while and then went back to Liberia to become Minister for Agriculture. Sadly he was later executed on the beach, with all his colleagues, by resentful northern rebels.

It was clear to me that I would, if I were not to spend endless hours gazing out of the windows at the spectacular scenery, have to develop my own work programme.

Adrian, my boss, was indeed a very lazy fellow and explained that the huge pile of unread reports on his in- tray ensured that any senior visitor would appreciate how overworked he was. Whenever I made suggestion of work he would suddenly interrupt, look out of the window and say: " Bridger, just look at those damn birds", as buzzards, or vultures, endlessly circled the town centre waiting for the all too ample supplies of carrion which littered the town centre.

Nevertheless he was not entirely negative and I was amazed and delighted when he agreed that we should publish "An Agricultural Economics Bulletin for Africa" on a regular basis, which we would circulate to all member countries – provided I could secure sufficient articles for the first three issues.

It took time to assemble, commission and write enough articles but I set to. I persuaded my boss to write one, and my colleagues were harried in the same way. We agreed to commission one of my ex lecturers at the LSE to visit West Africa and write up the experiences of irrigation in the French countries of the region.

I developed a particular interest in agricultural re-settlement schemes in Eastern Africa and he agreed that I could visit the countries to measure their success or failure. These schemes, which entailed transferring farmers to "new" areas, were popular with central planners and politicians but the complexities of them usually caused them to end in failure. After visiting and studying as many in Kenya, Uganda and Tanganyika as I could, I found one common theme for success. That was that the further the settler had come the greater the likelihood of success. In other words a settler was likely to make a far greater effort to achieve success if he had made a great effort to get there. On reflection this should have been blindingly obvious for "incomers", "foreigners", almost invariably bring with them the determination or indeed the desperation needed to succeed. One only has to look around the world to see the universal verity of this conclusion. Still I was quite pleased with this piece of micro socio-economic research and felt that had there been a Nobel Prize for pioneering research in that field it merited an award.

Once this exciting new publication was off the printing press I was despatched on a three month assignment to a yet-to-be- independent Tanzania to advise the Ministry of Agriculture on some economic issues. I suspect Adrian was delighted to get me off his hands for a while.

Dar-as- Salaam, the capital, was a steamy gem of a colonial capital. Palm trees waved over sandy beaches and an azure sea lapped a beautiful harbour. Splendid pre- First World War German timber buildings with wide verandas provided us with hot, shady offices. Neatly clad British Colonial Officers in immaculate shorts and long white stockings straight out of a "Sanders of the River" novel, epitomised the dying days of Imperial rule.

I was given a vacant District Officer's House to live in with my family, overlooking a splendid Indian Ocean beach and views of dhows quietly sailing past. The drive to work each day is still a glorious memory of palm-lined dazzling white beaches nurturing an azure sea with lazy dhows dotting the horizon.

My reception was not as enthusiastic as I had expected for my colleagues rather resented an "overpaid UN expert" being parachuted in. As I discovered later in other countries as well, this was a common and not wholly unjustified reaction and one had to work quickly and sensitively to overcome the resentment and prove that one respected their role and expertise – and of course had something new to offer.

My main task was to advise them what to do about a huge river basin study that had been published. River basin studies are very popular with irrigation engineers, politicians and international bureaucrats. They provide endless research opportunities and plenty of professional work while holding out to the electorates hopes of a transformed future.

In fact most of these projects ignored such economic realities as lack of large-scale markets, the problem of managing and allocating water efficiently, and successful new large-scale irrigation schemes are difficult to come by.

After visiting the area and not wishing to be too negative I recommended a very small pilot scheme with ten farmers. This modest approach was greeted with great relief as it suited the nervous Agricultural Department and I understand they implemented it in due course.

Back at the Commission, Adrian was still worrying about his "damn birds" and sheltering behind even larger piles of unread reports. He was obviously quite relieved when he was able to tell me that he had another job for me. The Ethiopian Ministry of Agriculture had failed to produce the Five Year Plan which the Yugoslav Economic Advisers in the Ministry of Planning had required of them a couple of years back. Would I help out? This seemed to me an excellent idea as the Ministry was just down the road and it would enable me to work with Africans for a change.

I joined a Committee, chaired by the Minister, which had about fifteen Ethiopian staff, an occasional Yugoslav from Planning and a US Economist from the USAID Mission. The Minister was a charming highly educated man but at a bit of a loss on how best to proceed. Mike, the US economist, overwhelmed us all by producing a splendid aerial survey of Ethiopia which USAID had flown at huge expense - but none of us were sure how we could use it. I do not think my questions to this effect pleased him, especially as he was not clear himself but thought that with all the aid the US was providing his role should be a key one. However, his main suggestion for transforming Ethiopian agriculture was – rabbits. The reasoning was that no other animal produced as much meat per unit of feed as rabbits, thus Ethiopia should solve its nutritional deficit by encouraging rabbit production. The polite disbelief on my colleague's faces as they listened to this advice was splendid to behold. I suspected that they, like me, had visions of millions of escaped rabbits eating up all the crops while desperate farmers were blasting away at them with their ancient guns It had the effect of ensuring that Mike played no role in the subsequent plan and left the field open to his hated rival.

I was able to devise a way of allocating the Ministry's scarce budgetary resources in a slightly more consistent and positive fashion by prioritising farm products most likely to generate greatest value added (mainly coffee) at the least possible cost, which seemed to satisfy the Minister. We even identified new Game and Forestry Reserves though this was "pie in the sky" as we were not able to visit the areas or involve any of the other parties. This was not quite true as I went to visit the Forestry Officer responsible for giving out timber permits in the forest .I leafed through his file and found quite a number of dollar notes which applicants had kindly given him as a bribe which he had forgotten about.

I was left to write the Plan and Adrian agreed to our UN Secretary typing it, as the Ethiopian Secretary's English was not good enough.

Meanwhile I had established an excellent rapport with the Minister and he would, to his subordinate's irritation (as they told me some years later when I visited them) call me in for advice from time to time.

On one occasion I mentioned that Jean had never met the Emperor and asked if he could arrange this, to which he happily agreed. Later the Minister called me back and asked if he could meet Jean and me at his office. He told us that he had arranged an audience with HIM but meanwhile he presented Jean with a gold broach of an Ethiopian shield and myself with an Imperial tiepin and cuff links. Jean was quite overwhelmed by her present, it was real gold.

Alas for reasons that were never explained, after we had left Ethiopia, I heard that the Emperor was displeased with the Yugoslavs and the Ministry Plan we had produced with them was shelved. But worse still many years later the kindly, educated Ato Bekele Selassie, the Minister with whom I had worked closely, was assassinated in a Cabinet room with twelve Colleagues.

REVOLUTION

I had been sent to the distant obscure country of Tchad, whose capital, Fort Lamy, conjured up legends of the Foreign Legion, together with a sophisticated Ethiopian, given to quoting TS Elliot, who said to me when he heard he was to come with me " Gordon, are there cannibals in Tchad?" We heard on the radio while at the conference that there had been a coup in Ethiopia and that the Emperor had been overthrown and his son the Crown Prince had taken over. The Emperor had been visiting Brazil and immediately flew back, by extraordinary coincidence stopping over at Fort Lamy on his way, but refusing to give us a lift home.

The Coup was eventually suppressed and several of his Imperial Guard who had led it were strung up in the main square.

However, having abandoned Jean, it was extremely worrying waiting for non-existent news in the middle of Africa. Having our house next to the army barracks did not, on reflection, sound a very good idea. Quite the reverse.

But let her tell her own story:

" I was sitting on the veranda at 11 am on Tuesday waiting for a visitor when Geraldine Amos (later becoming an eminent charity worker in the UK) and Bernard Chidzero (who become Minister of Finance in the new Zimbabwe Government) came zooming up the drive at a great pace .'Had I not heard? There had been a coup d'état the night before' and although all was quiet it might be an idea if Jeremy and I went to stay with Geraldine for a few days. Bernard drove off and Geraldine and I packed a few things, locked the house and off we drove. I drove though I had no driving licence; and had always been terrified of driving in Addis. I managed perfectly and now think I might apply for one.

The first day all was quiet but at the Amos' we felt quite excited. Next day we noticed a mass of armed soldiers pass the house on the way to the town but did not attach much significance to it as the day before soldiers filled the town. I thought we had better see that the house was OK and also collect our passports that I had forgotten. So Jim (Geraldine's husband, later to become a prominent Town Planner in Britain) and I set off in his Land Rover at about 2 pm. Our house was on the Bishoftu Road, and we had to pass under a narrow railway tunnel immediately after which is the largest army camp in Addis. Our house was about 300 yards beyond it.

We were stopped several times by armed troops on the road but Jim explained that "our house" was just up the road and we were let through.

Outside the Camp there were manned tanks. We got into the house and had just put the key in the door when all hell broke loose. We bundled the servants into the corridor and shuttered all the windows. It was rather like an air raid but with explosions and machine guns and even aeroplanes swishing down. Looking through the shutters we could see a tank just outside our garden about 40 yards away. There was hand-to-hand fighting all around the houses and later we found lots of spent bullets in the garden The water tank in the house next door was like a fountain having been penetrated by bullets.

We were resigned to having to spend the night in the house when at about 5.30 the fighting died down so we made preparations to go through the town. Jim put down the top of the Land Rover and the windscreen to make it look more civilian and I constructed a huge flag out of sheeting and drew a UN in eyebrow pencil on it and pinned it to a broomstick handle. We took Yeshie, the Nannie, in the back leaving the quaking sabanya (Mandivoro the watchman) to guard the house and drove as fast as we could. Outside the Army Camp we had to get out because of firing and zooming aeroplanes. There were many dazed civilians huddled against buildings and we saw some bodies being dragged into the camp.

We decided to continue along roads bristling with soldiers up the main avenue, Churchill Avenue. We were greeted by hundreds of Ethiopians who must have thought we were the Emperor's vanguard for they clapped and ululated, some even throwing themselves on the ground. Holding aloft this huge banner felt quite elated. We drove on to the United Nations HQ where all the staff was still cowering as it was badly damaged, being next door to the Ministry of Defence, which had been attacked by the rebels. One UN staff member was killed.

We collected Geraldine who was very surprised, seeing us like some modern day Boadicea with an unfurled white pillow case standing in a Land Rover, and asked how 'you could make ourselves look so ridiculous' - and we drove back to their home.

Fighting went on all that night and next day and all electricity went off. We lifted up the telephone and heard music, and then announcements that the Emperor had returned but the fighting continued and Jim decided to make a trial run to the Embassy but was turned back by heavy firing. Fighting went on over the city till Saturday when all went relatively quiet".

The Emperor's loyal army had suppressed the revolt by the Imperial Guard some of whom claimed that they thought they were opposing a coup.

It was not long before their leaders' bodies were swinging high in the main square.

TRAVEL AND TOURISM

It is difficult for anyone with a television screen, watching the hauntingly painful scenes of pot-bellied starving children, imagining Ethiopia as being anything but a bleak bare country abandoned by nature and neglected by God.

But the central plateau of this largely highland country is as beautiful and fertile as any landscape you can find. Particularly after the rains when the valleys are lushly green against a finely patterned horizon of blue hills and mountain peaks punctuated by trees and deep rushing rivers.

The horror stories, which are mainly true, are to be found in northern Ethiopia where spectacular canyons, in series after series, disappear into even deeper gorges with cultivated terraces clinging desperately to every reasonable surface, whose soils are gradually being carried away to sustain the huge populations on the River Nile.

These northern Tigrean areas have been for centuries a source of out-migration, as the soils simply cannot sustain much of a population. With masses of international food aid now being poured in, the population has stabilised and is even increasing - but only as a result of free food supplies, thus creating a massive commitment by the International Aid Community and a moral dilemma of monumental proportions. Does one continue food aid forever?

To the east the country dips down into the Danakil desert where an equally harsh desert environment provides for only a primitive nomadic way of life. To the south and west the plateau tails off gradually through coffee forests into a desert which allows for meagre subsistence agriculture and an impoverished population who served as the main source of slaves for the Arabian Gulf.

The paradox of the beauty of the highland areas and the often distressing poverty was not easy to comprehend, but it meant that beggars, almost unknown in colonial Africa, were a common feature of the urban landscape. Even in picturesque, seemingly fertile, rural areas, where one would stop for a picnic, we would soon be surrounded first by curious children and eventually adults asking for or hoping for presents of cast- off tins of food or even cartons and paper. One was never in a threatened situation but the haunting sight of these pathetic poverty-stricken bystanders always preyed on one's conscience.

LALIBELA

Our wheezy Dakota, with twenty United Nations staff aboard, skimmed over endless green pastures, alarming farmers, ploughing with ancient long wooden digging sticks and passengers as well, as we feared that the pilot was running out of fuel.

Just as we were bracing ourselves for a crash landing when we were within yards of the ground the land disappeared dramatically and we faced a dizzy drop into a deep canyon thousands of feet deep.

We then descended further and eventually found a grassy landing strip which the pilot bounced us onto. Disembarking with great relief we were met by around thirty saddled mules and as wild a desperate gang of bandits as one would see in an old Viva Zapata movie.

With wild, unkempt hair and beards, wrapped in dirty white shammas and dirty white leggings, some with shoes or some with bare feet, they were festooned with cartridge belts and carried large rusty old rifles. Their presence was explained as being our bodyguard to fend off rival bandits.

Clambering onto primitive wooden saddles we set off on what turned out to be a hair- raising three-hour stumbling mule trek on a steep narrow mule track which was strewn with stones, destroying one's belief in these supposedly sure footed animals. Along a good part of this dreadful track one peered over into a canyon, which would have meant instant death had we keeled over. In a few cases one was terrified to note that one's mule was stepping over deep crevices in the path.

The town of Lalibela consisted of two-storey thatched roof houses made of brick or mud separated by ragged tracks which might pass muster as roads. There was an empty town square on a steep slope where some six slender tents had been erected for our convenience, surrounded by a stockade to keep out curious inhabitants. The tents were supported by innumerable ropes, not all that robust as one, I noted, had been tied to a clump of grass.

There was great excitement from the huge crowd of poverty- stricken people who milled around us and who were kept at bay by our fierce, no nonsense banditti.

The 11 churches we had come so far to see were built in the 1twelth century and are unique in the world and thus not easy to imagine. Assume that you are standing on a level piece of ground. Imagine a square trench being dug about 30 yards deep and 20 yards. This then isolates a huge block of rock in the form of a square. This becomes the basis of the church. The interior is then excavated from the bottom and the interior shaped to create the church.

The interiors had very high ceilings. Some had windows and stairs, and the interior was decorated with primitive Coptic frescos.

While the exterior appearance of the churches was austere and generally devoid of much attempt at decoration, scarcely comparable to our great Gothic cathedrals, they were in terms of effort and scale an amazing achievement and an awesome sight. One large church had ten columns down each side carved into an original block, and was about the size of a large English rural church. Doors and windows and steps had been beautifully sculpted out of these great blocks of stone.

The impact of seeing these churches, and there was eleven of them, was quite stunning. They were built of fairly soft attractive pink tufa, and generally lacked decoration but one's reaction was of incredulity at the scale and the effort required to build them rather than being carried away by their aesthetic merit.

The guardians or priests hardly did credit to these stupendous creations. Desperately poor and shabbily dressed they showed us around the dim interiors. There were quite a number of early Coptic coloured frescos on the ceilings or the walls but of very elementary designs. Pictures of angels were in white - devils were painted black.

They anxiously took out an ancient Geez (the original language) bible, a manuscript bible that must have been a hundred years old, but as they roughly turned its pages it was dropped and split in half.

In the courtyard walls outside, tombs had been dug into the walls but they had not been properly maintained and had opened in some cases and human remains could be discerned. Near one church there were bones lying around in the courtyard.

All churches had a sanctuary to which access is forbidden but when briefly on my own I thrust aside a dusty curtain and peeked in – there was an old bicycle in it.

Everyone seemed to be asking for alms or "backshish". A sad looking man with anguished eyes approached and suddenly without warning pulled up his sleeve. His arm was a green gangrenous mess. I recoiled in horror. There was nothing I could do for him – no hospital within days - no medical help. I gave him some money but this would not save him.

We retired for the night to our flimsy tents and even flimsier beds. These, if they did not collapse ripped if one turned over, sharply depositing the occupants on the floor. The night was rent by canvas ripping, followed by loud cries by the woken sleeper and hysterical laughter from the rest of the campers. That night half of us slept on the floor.

We had further opportunities to see many of the other churches, participate in a church service before returning to the airstrip, most of us deciding to walk back rather than risk a mule. A splendid visit.

JIMMA

This capital of the south was the third town of Ethiopia and the centre of the huge wild coffee growing area of the south.

We drove down into the beautiful Omo Valley, up through hills bright with spring fields, patched with brilliant yellow noug plants, punctuated by trees of all shapes and varieties. The Blue Mountains and twisting roads reminded one of the "White Highlands" of Kenya, of the Eastern Highlands of Zimbabwe and even of Cumbria on a bright summer's day. The round neatly thatched houses complemented this lush environment and reminded one that an early British traveller described how under a wise Ras this had been a prosperous peasant community.

Our hotel in Jimma was surprisingly comfortable and we were amazed to find in a subsequent walk around the town that it had street lights, paved roads, sidewalks and for several hundred yards, arcades of shops.

A closer inspection revealed that the shops were shoddy and empty or converted to bars or brothels, the sidewalks untended, and there were many unfinished buildings which had been abandoned. Villas had been neglected and were overgrown. The airport still had the skeletons of five Italian Fiat aircraft on it, which had been destroyed by the British twenty years earlier

In most African countries this beautifully fertile area would have produced a bustling wealthy, new town - but we were told only two new buildings had been built since Italian times. We were shown round by the very frustrated and disgusted Israeli Chief Engineer for the town who said that it was almost impossible to get anything done because bribery was so widespread. Influential people just lived off bribery.

It was suggested that we should go and visit the Sultan of Kaffa who lived in a palace overlooking the town. Since he must be a descendant of the legendary rulers of medieval Kaffiria this seemed a splendid idea. He was, we were told, the grandson of the Sultan of Kaffir who had ruled independently over these fertile coffee and slave producing lands until Emperor Menelik 1 in 1890 "persuaded" him to become his subject.

The Palace was a long two- storey T- shaped wooden building with a spacious veranda all along the second floor and a corrugated iron roof, with a decorated third storey turret. The building was not exactly well maintained; it had not been painted for many years and looked decidedly crumbly. I noted that several of the timber uprights rested ingeniously on old car gear wheels.

The courtyard was bare and would have done credit to one from "Cold Comfort Farm" but the Sultan was obviously a man of wealth, as he owned a Jeep, clearly a left- over from the war.

The Sultan was tall, rather bulky amiable man who was quite cheered to greet unexpected visitors. He took us upstairs through many large empty rooms with wooden floors made of planks, which had been chiselled flat, with many mysterious large storage pots for treasure or maybe for storing crops.

His living room consisted of a huge four-poster bed with a pyramidical wooden ornament at each end into which many colourful tiles had been stuck. Adjoining it was his grandfather's very comfortable velvet-covered throne with huge, round velvet arms on which he sat. There was his father's huge wardrobe decorated with many tiny mirrors and a table with a teapot ingeniously shaped in the form of a duck.

He was quite delighted when we offered to take his photograph and hunted around desperately for his sword – which he could not find - though he did find a shield.

We exchanged many pleasantries but I refrained from asking him about the state of the town, slavery and what he thought of the Emperor. We departed promising to send him his photograph.

As we left, on the way out, being unnoticed, I could not resist lifting the cover of one of the pots. It was full of rusty bedsprings.

NAZARETH

Fortunately I was driving fairly slowly through this reassuringly named town, just 30 miles south of Addis Ababa when I ran her down. Dressed in shoddy white shamma she was very elderly by Ethiopian standards, she calmly walked in front of the car.

A huge crowd gathered round her inert body but despite shouts from Jean that I would get torn to pieces by a furious anti-"farenji" crowd if I left the car, I boldly stepped out to examine the damage – to the woman, not the car. However, they did not assault me and I suspect they were not much concerned, and they were even quite friendly. Fortunately a policeman unexpectedly turned up. We bundled this sad bag of rags into the back of the car and once again quite fortunately, we were told there was an American Mission Hospital nearby so I drove her there.

In response to my knock on the door of the Mission Hospital, an alert, middle- aged American surprisingly appeared. "Sorry to bother you," I said "I have an injured woman in the back of the car could you help her ?"

"Who's paying?" he demanded abruptly. Rather thrown by his priorities I replied; "She suddenly walked in front of my car, I was travelling pretty slowly, and it really was not my fault." "Bah," he said, "They all say that. I get lots of Italians who leave off injured people here and expect me to deal with them. I won't treat her till I am paid."

"I thought you were a Mission Hospital," I said fairly tactfully."What's that got to do with it?" he replied, "Someone has to pay." Rather baffled by his Missionary priorities I thought I had better excuse my ignorance of his medical problems by saying: "I have worked in many African countries and never come across a demand for payment by the authorities."

"That," he said, "is socialism." I was tempted to embark on a theological dispute about Christianity but replied: "Could you let me have the address of your head- quarters. I would like to write to them and tell them about your financial problems as they surely did not send you out here expecting you to get Africans to pay for treatment?" He did not appreciate my offer of help and replied, "Are you trying to make trouble?"

This interesting exchange was interrupted by groans from my elderly passenger so I thought I had better give in and say that I would make a contribution to her costs, which calmed him down and he agreed to treat her.

Unfortunately, the matter did not end there, as I was then obliged to attend a trial for having run her down.

I returned about a month later – with an agent, who thought that $10 compensation would probably settle the matter as she only had a broken leg. On arrival, my trial had to be adjourned for a couple of hours as the policeman could not be found, so while waiting outside in the car I had an opportunity of observing a slice of life in this biblically named town. Indeed it was probably not all that different in its buildings and its activities from its namesake.

It consisted of a collection of mud houses with either thatched or corrugated sheet iron sheet and a few shops in one main road, selling basic consumer goods, as well as some bars and brothels. The corrugated- iron roofs and the last facility were probably the only obvious differences from its historic counterpart.

It gave me a splendid opportunity to watch life in this tiny urban settlement. Trains of stately camels carrying salt from the Red Sea, textiles from Dire Dawa and charcoal from the forests, kept gliding by as if modern forms of transport had not yet been invented. Then all of sudden thirty chained prisoners appeared taking their daily stroll around the town before their incarceration. Then a gentleman with only a shirt on proudly appeared and bowed, in reverse, as he went past us. Then most remarkable of all, a very elderly lady appeared. She was sitting upright in an old wooden wheelbarrow pushed by a retainer and holding high a scarecrow umbrella. She looked very superior and dignified and was quite taken aback to see a car with us sitting in it. With an imperious wave she indicated to her retainer to reverse back to us and then thrust out a hand demanding alms.

Meanwhile my Agent told me that the woman's husband had been prepared to settle for $ 85 – which I would have been pleased to pay, but the Judge advised him that $ 200-300 would be better. Apparently the husband when finding that his wife was being treated at the Mission Hospital had taken her away and sought help from a local "doctor", who had removed her plaster cast and she was now seriously ill.

The Courtroom, about the size of a largish living room, had five rows of benches, a table on a dais where three judges sat and a witness box. One of the Judges had fallen asleep but was startled awake when I, a "feranji," came in. There were about twenty people attending a trial of a murderer who was squeezed into the witness box together with his two witnesses who were being cross-examined. Two "soldiers" loitered near the accused, one wearing sandals, the other puttees and boots, one in shorts, another in jodhpurs, and each with worn-out old shirts and different coloured berets to distinguish them from the rest. They both carried rifles which were obviously a great inconvenience as one of them left his on the floor while the other strung it round his back to the considerable inconvenience and danger of the witnesses and murderer he was guarding.

There was a continual hubbub and when the prosecutor could not be heard because of the noise outside he asked for it to be subdued so both "soldiers" rushed out leaving the murderer and his witnesses on their unprotected own.

My appearance led to the murderer's trial being interrupted. And the Prosecutor asked my agent "Why didn't your client treat the woman properly ?" This led to a very heated exchange between my Agent, the Prosecutor and the Judge, which I could not follow. My trial was interrupted from time to time by the murder trial, also the subject of much shouting. When it got back to me there was more shouting, my Agent telling me they now wanted $ 500 compensation, this being about 10 years income for a peasant, he thought they were going over the top. He was very angry indeed. After even more shouting, the Judge getting very excited, they settled for $200. It was a very interesting "Evelyn Waugh" experience.

FAREWELL

We had been in Ethiopia for just over two years when my ambitious nature led me to apply for a promotion within the United Nations in their prestigious Economic Commission for Latin America which was based in Chile. I was surprised when I was I was offered the post. So once more we were on our travels.

Before we left the Minister of Agriculture had kindly organised an audience with the Emperor for Jean and myself. He stood waiting at the end of a long 70 ft audience hall of the Palace. There was a warm red carpet spread over the floor and Victorian chairs and settees lined the side. Three huge paintings of Coptic ceremonies hung from the walls and three immense chandeliers with rows and rows of glittering reflective lights hung down the centre of the huge chamber.

The Emperor was only some 5ft 3in tall and dressed in a neat khaki uniform, splendidly set off by an array of brightly coloured decorations, looking rather more tired than his aristocratic beard and Semitic features should have allowed him to be.

His diminutive and passive figure belied the determination and skill which had enabled him to survive 50 years, ruling this wild turbulent medieval empire and seeking to modernise it. His appearance led his many enemies to underestimate his skill and determination to drag Ethiopia into the modern world; there had been many revolts, many attempts on his life, as he sought to abolish slavery, diminish the power of what we now call "war lords", introduce schools and build up a modern army and civil service for this poor, backward country. He made a speech of welcome to us all – his voice surprisingly deep for a small man and we later walked past and were acknowledged by handshake and a nod.

This was our farewell to Ethiopia and our last sight of this extraordinary monarch who lived to rule his country for some fifty years before being overthrown in 1974 by a coup led by the northern Tigrean people. He died in captivity in 1975, murdered by his captors.

Chapter Four

THE LAST COUNTRY IN THE WORLD

We were startled awake by a thunderous crash. The sound of a wardrobe keeling over? Then silence. We sat up in bed, searching for the bed lights. The lights revealed no sign of any collapse. Then we noticed it. A very gentle swinging of the ceiling light. We had experienced our first earthquake. This was just a gentle one - a tremor as the earth readjusted itself under our feet.

We were in Chile. It was the first of January 1963.

In 1835 the youthful intrepid Charles Darwin noted with perceptive puzzlement, while crossing the Andes, that at 14,000 feet there was a stratum of soil containing sea shells. How on earth had they got there? It took nearly a century for it to be explained that this immense Andean mountain chain had been created by the inexorable pressure from a tectonic plate gradually pushing against the coast of South America from under the Pacific Ocean.

This meant that Santiago, the capital of this remote country to which we had been posted, would inevitably end up several thousands of feet higher than it was at present. It was doubtful whether future travellers would come across a huge city balancing precariously on Andean peaks; more certainly they would witness with excitement a soil profile with myriads of shards and other man- made materials; a distant reminder that men's accomplishments are fragile. We hoped we would not be among them.

Reflecting on the brief, fleeting incidental nature of our life on the planet we could only console ourselves with the thought that the process would, we hoped, take at least a million or more years before it was likely to shift us that far. Although who knows whether we might at any time be submerged by a giant tsunami, or an earthquake at 9 on the Richter scale?

Reassured by the odds on our survival we went back to sleep.

CHILE

The title "The Last Country in the World" was one used by an eminent Chilean writer to explain its isolation at the other side of South America, separated from most of its neighbours by its spectacular mountain chain on the east, a bleak absolutely rainless Atacama desert to the north, an endless Pacific Ocean on the west and the stormy Cape Horn to the south.

It is perhaps a bit difficult to conceive of this title as relevant in the twenty first century. Santiago, the capital of Chile, is a frenetic centre, of many millions of people, with gleaming new cars, traffic jams and shining skyscrapers. Within a couple of decades, since the early 1980s, it has been transformed from a dull largely nineteenth[h] century Spanish town with aged American cars, into the Singapore of Latin America.

But Chile is still different and Chileans are still different from their Latin neighbours. Its early European population had originated largely from the northern mountains of Spain via a perilous journey across the Atlantic, through the tropical trials of Panama, and then down the coast to the jewel of the Spanish Empire, Peru. From there driven by desperation or wild hope, they traversed mountain ranges and deserts to discover, in central Chile, a temperate paradise of well watered fields, an El Dorado of agricultural plenty.

These settlers came largely from the north west of Spain: Galicians, Asturians, Basques, were hardy, thrifty peasant farmers with impossible names full of z's and y's, and were very similar to the thrifty peasant stock of north western Europe, and accustomed to tough agricultural work. They were quite different from so many of the conquistadores who migrated to Latin America from harsh dry semi-nomadic areas of western and southern Spain and who brought with them a feudal culture of fighting and dominance.

Having failed to enrich themselves with the gold and silver looted from the Incas in the high Andes of Peru and Bolivia, they settled in the fertile grape growing comfort of the river- strewn valleys of central Chile.

Isolated as they were for so many years they developed a sturdy sense of self- reliance and a sense of national identity which linked them more closely to the cultures of North West Europe than those of the Mediterranean. Unlike most other Latin American people who associated themselves with France or Italy, the Chileans related more closely to the quieter, if duller and less flamboyant, British culture.

And they settled a country with an extraordinary geography. It extends as thin as string of spaghetti for some 2,700 miles, as far as from London to Egypt, and it is seldom much wider than the distance from London to Bristol. The towering often snow- covered Andes, are almost always visible from all parts of the country and create a sense of safe, awesome isolation.

The northern areas are desert, the southern areas spectacular fjords terminating in the bleak windswept mountains of Cape Horn. In between there are forests, provinces with wet green, glistening, fields like Devon or Cumbria, and then the irrigated central valley of Chile with its incredibly fertile vineyards and its rich soils which make wine flow like water.

When one looks at a map of the world which indicates its natural regions, there are five with enviable "Mediterranean conditions", hot dry summers and cool wet winters - California, Southern Africa,

South West Australia, the Mediterranean and Central Chile. But Chile, with innumerable rivers created by the towering Andes has been able to convert most of this huge central valley into a well-irrigated agricultural paradise. As a result, grape yields are two or three times greater than those in France and Italy, and the rich soils produce a plethora of abundant fruit and vegetables.

Its isolation from the rest of the world meant that for several centuries this extraordinary country was a European backwater. It was not until the late nineteenth century that Chile started benefiting from developments in the rest of the world. Firstly, it was the Californian gold rush with its demand for labour and agricultural produce which Chile could meet, then later the discovery of nitrates and copper in the north (which led to Chile acquiring this area from Bolivia and Peru), which were the basis of its new wealth.

Independence from Spain had been achieved at the beginning of the nineteenth century thanks to an incredible military feat by the Argentine General San Martin, who crossed the precarious Andean passes with 5,200 men to defeat the Spanish armies in Chile. Then, in the early 1820s the Chilean fleet, led by that most extraordinary of all British naval captains, Thomas Cochrane (he was the original Captain Hornblower), ably supported by other British captains and sailors, swept the Spanish fleet out of the Pacific and ensured that Spain could not succour its distant Pacific Empire. Cochrane's most spectacular achievement was to capture the Spanish flagship which had taken refuge in the port of Callao, by a silent attack in rowing boats in the middle of the night, and sailing it out under the eyes of the incredulous Spaniards.

During the twentieth century the country had grown moderately prosperous largely thanks to its exploiting its huge copper and nitrate deposits. It was ruled by landed aristocracy who were reluctantly accepting the emergence of active, liberal urban political groups in the 1930s. Middle class Chileans, in the early 1960s when we arrived, were justifiably proud of the fact that some of their recent Presidents could safely walk the streets on their own.

Following policies of industrialisation and economic self-sufficiency, stimulated by the Second World War, large numbers of impoverished rural workers had moved into the towns and became an increasingly powerful political force. The gap between the wealthy aristocracy and this new deprived urban electorate was building up to an explosive situation which erupted a few years after we left in 1966.

But Santiago in 1961, when we arrived there, still had that air of distance from everywhere and of being at the "end of the line". The cars and buses were decades out of date, the architecture was solid, earthquake proof, turn-of-the century classic Spanish, dress for men was respectable 1930s style, and if anyone wondered what happened to old, out-of-date European and American films, here they were in Santiago de Chile.

GETTING THERE

It was one of the last great passenger liners which left from Tilbury Docks in London, in 1961, on the South Atlantic run. For nearly 100 years these powerful steamships had reduced the transport time, from the rich beef and wheat producing Pampas, from three months to three weeks.

We were lucky to get berths on her. We were transferring from Ethiopia to Chile. Meanwhile when we had been in Ethiopia, Jean had returned to her home in Teignmouth to have our second child. She was a little blonde whom we named Diana. Fortunately the United Nations were splendid employers. Not only were we allowed to travel First Class, but we were able to travel to Britain and from there by ship to Buenos Aires. This gave us a leisurely three weeks of escape from normal life.

We had a send off from the Thames docks in London by admiring envious friends and family, suitably entertained in our two Staterooms, the two children having spacious separate accommodation. One was reminded of those black and white movies in which transatlantic liners left Southampton amidst showers of confetti. Our departure was not quite as dramatic though we did manage a glass or two of champagne.

We then had leisurely days of idyllic climate, plenty of space, a nursery with a governess, more food then we had ever seen in our lives, and plenty of entertainment.

I could not help reflecting on my change of fortune and hoped that there were more competent sailors at the helm of our ship than was the case the last time I had been at sea.

But now here we were, twelve years later, in stupendous comfort, presumably with no amateurs steering the ship; leisurely days and quiet nights. We had a brief stopover at Rio de Janeiro, one of the most beautiful ports in the world with its tropical green mountains, elegant apartment houses and curving white sandy beaches - a gem of a port. Our blonde children were the object of everyone's attention wherever we went. Even small children ran after them with excited admiration.

At last Buenos Aires stood out on the skyline, rather like New York, on the flat brown, seemingly endless, watery plain, which is the estuary of the River Plate. I was home.

The return to Buenos Aires of the prodigal son, now thoroughly respectable with an English wife, two small children and a permanent United Nations job, must have been a great relief to my family and to some of my 14 aunts and uncles and to a few of my 52 first cousins. My student left wing political meanderings at the London School of Economics, probably misreported and exaggerated, had not always been appreciated by this very conservative community, and my subsequent departure to "darkest Africa" viewed with much alarm. Nevertheless here I was, respectable at last and welcomed home. I must say even I was a bit surprised by the turn that my life and career had taken.

After a pleasant stopover in Buenos Aires we set off on the final stage of our prolonged journey. We had decided to fly to Chile rather than go by train. Jean was prepared to brave the quicker alternative of an Air Chile flight rather than the dusty dramatic railway journey.

In those days planes did not fly over the Andes but through them, the 18,000 feet barrier was too high for propeller aircraft, so they made their way through the narrow Andean mountain passes.

Jean of a distrusting nature where heavier-than- air travel was concerned, had forgotten to take a nip of "the hard stuff" before boarding but managed to secure a comfortable row of seats next to the emergency door. "Look" she said with great alarm "the emergency door handle is tied up with rope." It did seem that under the circumstances this had not been an appropriate seating choice.

"What are you going to do about it?" she demanded. I had been a Boy Scout and had got awards for tying knots and it seemed quite secure as I pulled it. "Not that you fool," rather unnecessary language I thought. She turned on me as if it were my fault "Get the Captain." There was no Captain around but I was able to catch the eye of a remarkably pretty air hostess and I nonchalantly pointed out this little problem. She looked at it, pulled at the door as hard as she could and much to her surprise and mine it held firm. "Don't worry, sir, it's quite safe," she said and disappeared before I could ask for a change of seats.

Our flight confirmed her assurances for the door held firm and within a noisy clattering couple of hours we were over the endless flat green Pampas heading straight for the Andes. The pilot seemed to have found the right valley for suddenly we were skimming over snow-covered peaks and boulders almost close enough to touch. It was not a practical proposition to ask the pilot to fly a little higher, though no doubt the 120 passengers, who perished a year later on a flight over the Andes when the pilot miscalculated the height of the valley, wished they had done so. And one could not forget the Uruguayan rugby players whose plane hit the slopes leaving 46 hungry cannibals to survive alone for nearly six months.

Then way down below us appeared the lush rich green tree lined valleys of central Chile.

We had arrived.

LIVING IN CHILE

This really was, in many ways, a dream assignment. Santiago was a dull, unimaginative sort of town. It was built on the traditional Spanish grid pattern and its solid earthquake-proof buildings and Colonial Plazas had little architectural merit.

However, the northern residential suburbs consisted of elegant, extravagant and imaginative villas set in fresh, beautiful gardens amidst acacia, jacaranda and poplar lined avenues.

We settled into a newly built "estilo ingles" three bedroom house, with external timber beams and inconveniently small triangular glass windows, but with a superb view over the Andes.

While our environment was one about which we could only have one complaint, (earthquakes), our financial circumstances, which we had thought were comfortable enough on United Nations terms in Ethiopia, were even better because of the economic conditions in Chile and the United Nations concessions we enjoyed.

The Chilean Government had for years been pursuing a policy which ensured that its foreign exchange rate was held down which meant that there was a huge black market for foreign currencies, and especially US dollars, in which we were paid. The local Escudo was seldom worth much more than one third of a US dollar so that anyone selling dollars on the black market could get as much as three times its official value.

When I went to cash my first salary cheque drawn on a US bank at the local bank, my colleagues were aghast "Nobody," they stated in unison, "but nobody changes at the official rate." Indeed I found this was so. Even personal cheques signed by the United Nations

Representative to Chile, with his signature, which he had changed on the black market were being exchanged in the black market and could be cashed at several times the official rate. This dual exchange rate, an official and a black market rate, was unofficially accepted by the Government and they made no attempt to clamp down on it. There was nothing for it but for me to conform.

Furthermore, there were other financial benefits from being a U.N. employee. We were exempt from national taxation. And since Government policies had instituted high import taxes to protect the local economy and raise revenue, we could import U.S. goods duty free.

As a result if every UN employee did not have a Sears Roebuck catalogue, their wives would. This tantalising access to the greatest consumer-durable economy in the world did, in my opinion, often occupy too much of colleagues, time. While I do not think anyone abused their privileges by setting up "businesses", at least not obviously so, a good deal of time had to be spent negotiating goods through the Customs House bureaucracy, time which should have been spent on international public duties.

But the greatest UN perquisite was permission to import a car duty free every two years. It could be, and was, sold after two years. Since the Government had a massive import tax on cars, such was the demand for them from wealthy Chileans, that after two years one could expect to "dispose" of it for at least three times the original price.

I noticed as a result that almost all my colleagues had a Mercedes Benz as these were in huge local demand and yielded the highest return to the fortunate importer. Unfortunately for me, I had not the funds on arrival to buy a Mercedes and had to settle for a mere Chevrolet station wagon, with enough space for a children's playground in the rear.

The impact of this new financial regime on one's budget was such that one could not be other than grateful.

Not surprisingly we settled into our new environment comfortably enough. We conformed to the social norm of employment creation and engaged a cook and a nanny, though heaven knows how they kept themselves occupied in a three-bedroom house. We did however, reduce the high unemployment rate by two.

Then the scenery. This was superb. The climate was excellent in summer with a cloudless blue sky and cool temperatures – though winters could be cold bleak and very rainy.

The staff we employed enabled Jean to embark on an arts course at the Academy of Fine Arts of the University of Chile.

Visits to the coast were frequent. The rugged and beautiful, sandy-rock- strewn coast line was touched with Mediterranean splendour and with wild bright yellow California poppies. Elegant villas had been built as summer resorts by wealthy Chileans and sandy beaches provided restaurants serving splendid fish dishes which would be washed down with wine costing little more than water.

There was, alas, always that downside; earthquakes. Mostly these were just in the form of minor tremors with an occasional loud crack and a gentle shake. All this reminded us that those tectonic plates were adjusting gradually and we therefore should not worry. But every time it happened one would wonder if it was the "big one" and one looked for a door arch and the children.

We experienced two severe earthquakes. Jean, with the children, was on the eighth storey of a building which started gently swaying and she had, for some two minutes, to negotiate her way down the stairs from the top of it.

On another occasion we were on a boat trip off the coast and saw people running away from the beach. Our boatman made for the shore at once and since the sea had not retreated as a result of an undersea earthquake, we sat in our car listening to almost hysterical radio broadcasts. They were filled with dramatic calls from Santiago, which was about 50 miles away, the broadcaster describing how the city had disappeared in a cloud of dust. He announced that electricity and telephone lines had been severed and fire engines were rushing around the city. One got the impression that it had been totally destroyed.

The official radio broadcasters were desperately trying to establish where the epicentre was but had to rely on ham radio as all normal communications were cut. It was fascinating, not to say alarming and exciting, to listen in to these calls from desperate radio operators. After about an hour they were able eventually to locate the epicentre which was mercifully some 60 miles north of the capital.

Eventually things calmed down and we drove off to visit the city. It had not disappeared in an enormous calamity but the falling debris had hidden the city in dust from which it now miraculously emerged. We did not see any collapsed buildings in the town centre but the roads were littered with broken rubble. There were many cracked walls and buildings but it was only in the poor areas where there were collapsed houses, all built of adobe.

Overall in quite a large region, 300 people lost their lives, 200 as a result of a dam breaking. The rest died in the poor suburbs where buildings were not earthquake -proof.

Just a small earthquake in Chile

While we did not allow this aspect of Chilean life to worry us unduly we did think from time to time how nice it would be to live in an earthquake-free country.

Because of its elegant elongated geography we were not able to make many trips southwards or northwards. We did take off once to the south through "endless" forests to the southern Lake District, a solid two-day journey, about as far as Gibraltar is from London. It was a land of azure lakes, and glistening green paddocks, amongst dripping wet trees, set against the spectacular snow- capped Andean mountains.

One was reminded of a pre-industrial Cumbria or Devon, untouched by the twentieth century. After torrential rains came glistening sunlight, on green fields. And one would come across stately horsemen, "Huasos," as they were called in Chile, "Gauchos" in Argentina, dressed in thick woollen tent like ponchos, and here and there one would find woodmen's cottages out of a Grimm's fairy tale. Most peasants lived off the trees from the forests and one passed, along narrow roads, oxen lethargically pulling creaking wooden carts on two huge solid wooden wheels carrying 50 foot poles, dragging them to local factories for processing.

Fascinated by these home-made solid wooden wheels we stopped at a woodman's cottage where one had been abandoned and asked if we could buy it. The owner's astonishment as he looked at this huge modern automobile which appeared to have all its own wheels was only overcome by the joy of being offered £1 for this abandoned wheel. This splendid piece of rural history accompanied us back to England and now resides in an agricultural museum in Surrey.

The most spectacular of all our trips was through the southern Andes to Argentina, which involved four lake crossings, three buses, and a stop at a hotel mid-way. We had great luck and had sparkling spring weather throughout the trip. It was a glorious travel feast of violent coloured plants and bushes on blue-green lakes squeezed between towering mountains. We were indeed fortunate to encounter two clear days for this splendid traverse.

Travelling right to the south of Chile is, or was, another matter. Punta Arenas, originally Sandy Point, named by Captain FitzRoy (of Darwin and "Voyage of the Beagle" fame), is just one of the British legacies of names to almost every inlet, bay and mountain in the southern tip of the continent. In the nineteenth century he surveyed, over two years, every nook and cranny of this amazingly complex archipelago on behalf of the British Government.

In the very south of Chile there is an increasingly popular National Nature Reserve, which is based upon the three spectacular needle-like mountains called Torres del Paine, the highest of which was only climbed for the first time in 1963, by Chris Bonnington. The Reserve attracted Jean's attention and she decided to abandon her family responsibilities and together with a friend flew south for a four- day escapade to this remote legendary attraction.

She had been preceded by a party of adventurous English aristocrats. In 1878, Lady Florence Dixie, accompanied by such famous names as Lord Queensbury, Lord James Douglas, Max Beerbohm's father who was an artist and who had visited western Patagonia (and was prepared to return despite having been captured by Indians on his first visit), by her husband and her two brothers. She was intrigued by this remote "outlandish out of the way place – land of the Giants and the golden city of Manoa" and organised the expedition.

They only took one servant as "English servants prove a nuisance and hindrance on expeditions of this kind which entail a great deal of roughing has to be gone through as they have an unpleasant knack of falling ill at inopportune moments."

Disembarking at the dreary settlement of Sandy Point they hired 50 horses and four guides to lead them over 300 miles of the Torres Del Paine to their mysterious mountain objective.

Their trek was by no means comfortable and their English servants must been grateful that they were not selected to join this spirited gang. The party was nearly burned to a frizzle in a grass fire and only miraculously escaped death by charging through it, as luckily they found a sandier area which was not burning so fiercely. Then they went hungry for several days as guanacos and ostriches who were their source of meat decided that these intruders were to be avoided. When they at last shot an unsuspecting guanaco they develop a relish for boiled guanaco- head soup.

On another occasion they were nearly left horseless two hundred miles from their base when a wild stallion attempted to seduce all their mares while they were away from their camp. It was only driven away at the last moment as they were returning.

As they penetrated more deeply into the Andes they entered areas so remote that guanaco, deer and birds were quite fearless of them and approached them with quiet, innocent curiosity. One can scarcely believe that our intrepid explorer excitedly shoots a friendly deer that comes to investigate her. However one's indignation is somewhat mollified when she admits the enormity of her action. She writes "I was haunted by a sad remorse for the loss of that innocent and trusting life", and the party gave up the unsporting shooting of such trusting creatures; well, at least until meat supplies became scarce.

After many hardships they are eventually rewarded by the sight of the Torres del Paine and she writes "the three red peaks and the Cordilleras – their white glaciers, with white clouds resting on them, were all mirrored to marvellous perfection in the motionless lake, whose crystal waters were of the most extraordinary brilliant blue I have ever beheld - the spirit of silence and solitude, that for a long time we stood as if spellbound none of us uttering a word."

On their return journey all their tents got blown away in one night of torrential rainfall, and then they went nearly three days without food, for again none of their sources of food waited around to be shot.

Lady Florence Dixie's book, when published must have been a great success. Even to-day it is a superb adventure story and one hopes that her companions enjoyed their adventure as much as she did.

Fortunately for Jean and her friend, technology enabled them to undertake a less arduous journey. They flew to the now- named town of Punta Arenas in a mere four hours. They were able to glimpse many of the brilliant blue lakes which so excited Florence Dixie from the air. "We flew over hundreds of lakes of all sizes shapes and colours. Some were lime green, brilliant blue, brown, yellow and grey – the coast line splintered with thousands of islands - green in the north and then further south mountainous, icy and barren," Jean records.

Punta Arenas now resembled a town, but not of the sort one wished to stay in so they made their way quickly in a crowded bus on a four hour journey to Puerto Natales where there was a hotel. They only had one day to see the fabled Torres so negotiated with a taxi driver to drive them the 80 miles to see them through the green rolling countryside backed by the "fabulous Darwin Mountain range".

"Where are the mountains?" enquired Jean of the taxi driver as they reached their cloud covered destination. "There they are senora –in front of you." But sadly Jean said "In front of there is nothing but clouds."

They returned dejected.

WORKING IN CHILE

The United Nations Economic Commission for Latin America (ECLA), which I had joined, had established for itself a considerable reputation as being the think tank, the policy forger, of the international "left" of Latin American countries. It had become a haven for left wing economists critical of capitalism, the USA, and of the International Monetary Fund.

Its basic policies were founded on the belief that central planning was essential to ensure an efficient and fair society and that the world's primary producers were at a permanent disadvantage against the industrialised countries because the demand for the basic primary commodities would not increase as rapidly as the demand for industrial products

They therefore promoted twin policies of central state planning and of economic self- sufficiency through high tariff walls and import restrictions, in order to promote and protect local industries.

Actually Latin American had been obliged to pursue these policies during the Second World War simply because international trade was interrupted. Many countries therefore found it essential to promote the production of local resources and restrict consumption of scarce expensive imports.

Unfortunately Latin American Governments pursued both policies with excessive zeal.

The ECLA doctrine gave legitimacy to these policies. Yet both were disastrous for the long-term economic and social welfare of Latin America. This was because central planning becomes increasingly difficult as economies became richer and consumers, in democratic societies, wanted more choice. It led to massive planning errors and misdirection of resources, which in other more democratic regions were overcome by shifting more decisions to consumers via market freedom.

However, in dictatorial societies these policies were a heaven- sent opportunity for a ruling few to control the economy of the country and consolidate their power and privileges. The communist centrally planned economies of Eastern Europe were the worst examples, but the many corrupt dictatorships in Latin America also benefited from central planning by being able to enrich themselves and their immediate adherents through rake-offs on the granting of permits for imports, exports, and local industries.

The second plank of Latin American policy, that of striving for economic self- sufficiency by restricting imports or imposing huge duties on them, led to the emergence of local industries and activities which were extremely uneconomic and expensive to local consumers. They required massive protection and direct or indirect subsidies which had to be paid dierectly or indirectly by a not very efficient exporting agricultural sector.

This policy led to expansion of urban areas, particularly capital cities, and created a demand for labour which attracted the rural workers to them. The workers then became politically powerful pressure groups working either for the State or for highly inefficient industries protected from foreign competition by import controls or very high tariffs.

This made the emergence of a more efficient market economy politically very difficult as it would entail State employees and workers in over- protected industries losing their jobs. Without welfare systems to cushion the unemployed, change became politically and economically difficult.

Most Latin countries were (and still are) struggling to overcome this legacy; up to half the population in some countries has now settled around the capital city. However, it was not in my humble role to challenge the eminent intellectuals of the ECLA who promoted it. I worked in the ECLA Agricultural Division managed by a very pleasant Chilean boss.

Unfortunately my new boss seldom emerged from his office. On one occasion when he did not appear for several days we knocked on his door to find he was not there; he had gone on an overseas visit but had not told us. Nevertheless he always seemed to be busy writing reports when he was in the office. His activities, we surmised later, must have been linked to his appointment to the left wing Allende Government, which was elected to power a few years later.

Once again one was left very much on one's own to produce reports, about the state of agriculture in Latin America, for the many conferences which delegates were supposed to read, digest and apply. Unfortunately reading these reports was time consuming and the purpose of most delegates at conferences, apart from collecting their huge per daily expense allowances and going shopping, was to make a speech which might attract headlines back home. Reports were seldom read and not much notice was taken of them.

In order to overcome boredom, and on my own initiative I carried out a study of the costs of farm machinery imports in Chile. This brought out the fact that importers' monopolies were able to charge far more, easily twice as much as farmers paid in other developing countries for the same machinery. This pleased my left wing boss no end and I have an uneasy feeling that this research may have been a factor in catapulting him, after I had left, to being appointed agricultural import controller by the socialist Chilean regime.

Because all countries had to produce a Plan if they wanted to secure foreign aid, a good deal of ECLA effort was put into economic planning to help these countries. This condition, curiously, had been imposed by that bastion of free enterprise, the USA. Accordingly large numbers of economists were employed drawing up such plans. Almost all were highly academic, prepared largely by academics or remote bureaucrats employing doubtful or just invented statistics which purported to prove that only a huge injection of foreign aid could create economic growth.

Since my Chilean boss had some requests pending for assistance from governments on how best to implement their paper plans in the agricultural sector, I was despatched to Bolivia, with a Chilean colleague, to advise their Ministry of Agriculture how to carry out a development plan which had been approved five years earlier but which had yet to be acted upon.

My experience in Africa inclined me to a more practical than theoretical approach and I had devised a system of "points planning" which was based on the facilities or resources a government department had available and the main activities (crops and livestock) they were likely to be able to promote. We quickly established a simple programme of work priorities for the Ministry.

Somewhat to our surprise, the US Economics Professor who was advising the government told us to take action and start implementing the programme. We only had a few days left so we hurriedly called together a meeting of all those in the government likely to be involved in the development of Bolivian llamas and guanacos , a key form of transport, wool and meat for Bolivian peasants. Great was the excitement of experts from Ministries of Agriculture, of Livestock, of Cooperatives, of Finance, of Economics when they met together. Their enthusiasm was amazing. They told us they had never ever met before and were thrilled at this novel way of planning. We set out an Agenda (also new to them) and a plan of action (also new to them). We departed heroes to these new converts to cooperative action.

Our report went down well with my new boss and I was then despatched to Paraguay to do a similar job. I did not have the courage to tell him that word had leaked back to us from Bolivia that the Minister of Economics was most upset to hear that his staff were collaborating with the Ministry of Agriculture, and had forbidden their participation in this "new" approach.

Paraguay was fascinating. This remote, isolated and verdant country had been cut off from most of its neighbours since its earliest days. The Jesuits had done a splendid job Europeanizing the Indians but resentful Spanish colonists had ejected them in 1767 because they had become too powerful and had hindered the enslavement of Indians.

Then they had a whole series of dictators who cut off Paraguay from their neighbours and even went to war with all three of them in the 1860s losing 70% of the male population in the resulting conflict.

Asuncion, the capital, was a hot, sticky but attractive colonial relic. Because the mid-day heat made it exhausting even to think, work started at 6.30 am and finished at 11.30 am. But the town was delightful in the cool evenings with long drawn-out dinners and strolling musicians playing the beautiful Paraguayan harp, which the Jesuits had introduced 200 years earlier.

Paraguay is the only country in Latin America in which the original native language, Guarani, is an official language. This unusual situation occurred because the Guarani Indians settled on rich fertile soils which easily met all their basic needs. This allowed a settled rather than nomadic way of life, and the Spanish conquerors intermarried with the local population at an early stage in the conquest.

The Paraguayans were somewhat better organised than the Bolivians, no doubt a continuous succession of dictators had created a better sense of order than was the case in Bolivia, so my task was a bit easier.

My task was to advise the Planning Board how to prepare investment projects for funding. My proposals that they should establish priorities, prepare a work programme, allocate responsibilities and set time schedules, were greeted with great surprise and enthusiasm. In most Latin Countries the basic principles of good administration: agendas, records, filing and recording let alone arriving for any meeting on time, were unknown , and extremely frustrating to those of us accustomed to assuming a reasonable administrative capacity . It was, of course easy to give sensible advice but there was little assurance that this advice would be taken.

I was later sent in early 1965 on a mission to the country of my birth Argentina, to advise on Agricultural Planning. Argentines possess a generally high level of education, great energy, and great individualism and have a high opinion of their own worth which most other Latins do not share. I was most impressed when I met the Head of Agricultural Planning. He told me that he had already produced a Plan and therefore had no need for my advice. To confirm this he presented me with a huge document full of impressive five-year forecasts of income and expenditure. I had never come across such a thorough, consistent piece of work and was quite stunned by its skill and diligence.

I asked him how he had organised such an impressive piece of work. "How many Committees had been set up, how many experts had he called in?" "Oh" he said proudly "I did it all myself."

One cannot think of better example of the difficulties and futility of State planning in Latin America.

Meanwhile, my personal odyssey, my ambitions, still ground on. I had served two years in Chile and swapped the Chevrolet for a Mercedes Benz. I now decided to apply for an upgrade and a new job, still within the United Nations family in Chile. This, if secured, would mean a promotion and a transfer, but still in Chile, to the Food and Agricultural Organisation (FAO) of the United Nations with its HQ in Rome, rather than my current employers whose HQ was in New York. If one was to have a longer term career, a posting to Rome sounded much better than one to New York.

The post I applied for was that of Regional Agricultural Marketing Officer for Latin America. The continental geographical scope sounded grand but the technical knowledge required seemed somewhat beyond me. However, I spoke Spanish, and bilingual professionals were scarce, and I had a fair amount of experience of marketing policy and marketing institutions. I must say I was rather surprised, and so were my colleagues, when I got the job.

I was still based in Chile, but I was mostly my own boss responsible only to a very pleasant German superior based in Rome. He had visited us in Chile and had met Jean and had impressed her no end when he said he knew her home town in Teignmouth, in south Devon, very well. When he explained, with some embarrassment, that he actually only knew it from the air her enthusiasm for him waned as she had had many German "visits" during the war and had been nearly blown up by one of them.

My new job entailed travelling around Latin America dispensing advice to governments on agricultural marketing issues. Unfortunately advice is seldom eagerly listened to, or ever taken up, because to do otherwise would reflect on the recipient's failure to anticipate it, and would affect someone adversely. This certainly applied to agricultural marketing systems and policies, however tactfully suggested. Since there were no financial aid inducements available which United Nations staff could offer, being an Advisor was a frustrating business.

It might be thought that travelling around the many exotic countries of Latin America at public expense was rewarding in itself. It is true that on weekends being on my own I would take off to some remote spot in interesting areas but travelling on one's own was a lonely business. The hospitality shown to visiting experts was almost non-existent. In any case, it conflicted with family life as I was supposed to spend about 50% of my working time away from home. My frequent disappearances were disruptive to home life (despite returning loaded with exotic gifts) and I came to realize the considerable drawbacks to the job I had undertaken.

My rank and experience meant that I was asked to participate in Project Identification Missions for the World Bank and Inter American Bank Project Identification Missions from time to time. These were interesting. On one them I had to go to Rome to complete the report which enabled me to pay a visit to London, where the British Government had established a Ministry of Overseas Development and I happened to know their new Chief Economist. As luck would have it they were looking for a Senior Economic Adviser for their Latin America aid programme and I was offered the post. The salary by British standards was excellent but nothing like the income my new FAO role gave me.

I had to weigh up the benefits of a permanent extremely well paid, but very unrewarding job, which entailed a great deal of travel, living in an attractive country with good promotion prospects to Rome or New York, against a far less well- paid job but a far more satisfying one in Britain.

The advantage of working for the British Government was that it had a substantial financial aid programme as well as providing technical advice, and therefore work was likely to be much more professionally fulfilling than working for the United Nations. Furthermore, as the children grew older there were surely advantages in entering them into the British educational system, and establishing oneself and family in a more permanent environment?

Should I abandon this "golden cage"? It entailed a big cut in income and abandoning hope of promotion to Rome or New York. What if the British Government, whose economic difficulties were well known, decided to cut its aid programme?

After careful consideration, together with Jean, I decided to ask for a one year leave of absence from the United Nations .If the British Government job did not work out, well, I could return to Chilean and UN comfort.

To my surprise the Head of FAO in Latin America agreed to this request, but to my extreme embarrassment I discovered that he had proposed to the British Government that in exchange for this 'generous gesture' on his part that they should support his candidature for the Directorship of the FAO, which was being hotly contested at the time and for which he was a leading candidate. I can imagine the polite incredulity of the British official who was canvassed in this way but it had no effect on the process of Britain's choice; they supported another candidate.

LOOKING BACK

Fortunately for me the vote was not known till after I had left Chile. It was therefore with many regrets that we left a beautiful country, an over paid job and many good friends, for Britain in 1966.

As has occurred all too often with countries in which we lived, Rhodesia, Ethiopia and Chile, it was not long before political and economic disaster overtook them.

The Christian Democrats who had pursued slightly left-of-centre policies were ousted from government and a Socialist regime (described by the right as Communist) came to power. It was the first time that a Socialist/Communist Government had been elected to power in the democratic world and great was the excitement of left-wing idealists and the Soviet Union and Fidel Castro.

Fidel Castro turned up and for three weeks harangued Chileans on how to transform the country into a Socialist paradise. The Soviet Union offered aid. While the social objectives, that of ensuring a better share-out of wealth were both understandable and commendable, the process by which the new regime of President Allende sought to achieve this was economically disastrous.

To embark on a wholesale reconstruction of the economy, and indeed of society, when only a third of the population had endorsed such a policy at the election, the other two parties splitting the vote, might seem unwise and unjust. Yet it might have been acceptable had it worked. But it did not.

The nationalisation programme of enterprises, land reform, price controls, central planning, all were mismanaged and were economically disastrous. Production collapsed, inflation became rampant. Scarcity of consumer goods brought house- wives out onto the street and factory workers often had to be paid in kind from the output of their own factories as money became valueless.

The USA meanwhile did everything possible to topple this anti-US regime. Their most effective intervention was to support transport workers financially who had gone on strike and paralysed the economy. Yet the US intervention was, as seems so often the case, mostly counterproductive, as the regime would have collapsed without their intervention, but it gave the supporters of the regime justification for its failure and the claim that they were victims rather than creators of that failure.

The military ultimately intervened and overthrew the regime and the President committed suicide in the process.

Never was the saying "He who sows the wind reaps the whirlwind" more apposite. The ferocity with which the new regime, under President Pinochet, intervened was unexpected and most would say out of keeping and unjustified in terms of the character and history of Chilean society. It has been estimated that between two and three thousand opponents, those who did not flee, were killed. Pinochet's supporters, those whose lands, factories and businesses were confiscated and then found that compensation was, if paid, in near valueless inflated currency, would have felt little compunction in justifying the terror which resulted.

It was on the basis of this national Chilean catastrophe that phoenix-like, a private enterprise economy emerged which has created the modern dynamic twenty- first century Chilean society – a system, which while chaotic, in many ways is more suited to the individualism and entrepreneurial dynamism of Latin American culture and temperament, than the centrally planned economies which have performed so poorly all over the world.

Chapter Five

BACK TO ENGLAND

The election of a Labour Government in 1965 brought to an end the rule of the "aristocratic" Conservative Party, and was a social revolution born of the Butler Education Act of 1944, grammar school opportunities for less wealthy families, and the boost the post war Labour Government gave to education.

An important social concern of the new Government was international poverty and the granting of independence to the declining number of colonies. This resulted in the creation of a Ministry of Overseas Development, established under Barbara Castle, one of the most dynamic of Government Ministers. She brought in Andrew Cohen, an energetic, liberal larger-than-life colonial civil Servant, as her Permanent Secretary, and an eminent left wing economist, Dudley Seers, as Director General of Economics.

Dudley recruited a large number of economists who, it was hoped, would inject the element of "development" into the new Ministry.

I had met Dudley in Ethiopia and Chile, so I had dropped in on him when on a mission to Geneva from Chile, and was offered the post of Senior Economic Adviser for Latin America. It was as simple as that; no interview board. I thought I had better mention that M I5 had their eye on me because of my student past but this did not bother him at all. Indeed I suspect he thought it was a commendation.

SETTLING IN

Jean and I returned to England in January 1966, a cold bleak year. We quickly found a house in the then smallish market town of Guildford. Its attractive cobbled High Street, easy access to open countryside, supply of good schools, being a thirty-five- minute train ride to London, and halfway between Heathrow and Gatwick airports, made it a very attractive location.

While the salary I was offered was a substantial one by British standards, it was only about half of my UN salary, and when one took into account that there were duty- free perks and no UK tax in the U.N., it was only about a third. However, it was equivalent to 50% of the cost of a three bedroomed house close to the town centre. Anyone today would have to pay about eight times as much for the same house.

I had persuaded Jean that our move to England was a good move as "man did not live on Mercedes Benz alone"; a generic aphorism which she maintained was gender biased and did not apply to her. She did not think it a good reason, not for her anyhow, for abandoning the good life, especially as our next move could well be to Rome. However, she agreed eventually to the move, as education of the children was a consideration and the profits we made (quite legally) from selling our beautiful white Mercedes for three times what we paid for it, enabled us to pay for our Chilean nanny to come back with us to England.

So we settled into a comfortable house overlooking Guildford. This site was to have a profound impact on our lives over the next 30 years.

THE MINISTRY

I could not believe my luck. I was working in an environment where everyone turned up to meetings on time. If one was a minute late, frowns all rounds. And there was a Chairman and an Agenda at meetings. The discussions were orderly and minuted. What a relief after working in Latin America where no one ever arrived on time, meetings were late, people walked in and out and one never knew what had been agreed.

Furthermore, incoming letters and reports could easily be found as there was a "Rolls Royce" registry system. Every letter that arrived was put in a file and entered on a blank sheet, on the other side of the file. All comments and advice would be recorded for the administrator responsible to deal with it. This simple system was splendidly effective. It was unbelievably simple and very efficient.

Then I was allocated a large enclosed office, no open plan, where one could work happily without interference. The post came with a Personal Secretary. Fantastic!

There were two other great advantages in working for the Ministry. The first was that one was free from ideological pressures which, alas, in the United Nations played an important part in one's professional work. In Latin America it was socialism and anti- North Americanism which determined one's effectiveness, and in Africa socialism and anti-white rule. In the Ministry it was facts which were important, not ideology. One usually won an argument with facts but it was a bit alarming, however, to find how easily non- economists would crumble under an array of them, for as every economist, knows there are "lies, damned lies and statistics".

Another great advantage was that the clear and settled staff hierarchy meant that no time was spent struggling for preferment. One could not influence the few opportunities for promotion which arose as one could in the private sector or in the United Nations.

There was a downside however; all the power lay with the administrators. Economists and other professional staff, such as agriculturalists, engineers, lawyers, were only advisers.

The great divide in British education, and indeed in British society, that of the "two cultures", was reflected in the British Civil Service where administrators with a background in classics or arts managed the Civil Service, advised by an array of experts who, denied management responsibility, had no experience in dealing with political, social or administrative problems. Their advice was therefore not always relevant and sometimes not understood by the decision- makers The weaknesses of the system had long been appreciated and the Government had published a report (The Fulton Report) which recognised the need for reform and visualised that a stronger professional element was needed in administration. This was discreetly resisted by administrators, who would lose out, and by many professionals who did not want to assume management roles. The introduction of the report was a very slow process taking decades to implement.

Meanwhile one had to cope with administrators, some of whom were hostile to economic advice and others who did not recognise the need for it. Occasionally I was unfortunate enough to be landed with an administrator who lacked "development interests" or skills. On the other hand there many who were excellent. On the whole the system worked well and if one encountered unreasonable obduracy one had the possibility of raising matters at a higher level.

It must be admitted, however, that unrealistic economic advice was often given to administrators, advice which they could not possibly take for administrative, social or political reasons. Academic economists had a more difficult time coping with these "practical" problems than those who had more direct experience of real life.

DEVELOPMENT POLICIES

The basis of the Government's policy was in principle to help countries to help themselves. To use jargon common at the time, the objective was "to assist countries to take off into self-sustained growth". In order to achieve this Holy Grail, countries had to make most of the effort themselves. It required stability, appropriate policies, energy and efficiency, and a measure of social and administrative integrity.

The objective of the Ministry was to provide the tools, the capital equipment, which developing countries would become responsible for maintaining. This was the concept: that it was better to assist people by giving them a fishing rod, rather than a fish. However, there were many colonies in receipt of annual budgetary subventions which was in conflict with our policy when the Ministry was first established. One of the main policies of the Ministry was to eliminate these as quickly as possible. By the early 1970's this had largely been achieved.

One of the major problems I encountered with the administrators, or desk officers, dealing with country programmes was that they had no experience of what "development" entailed. For almost all desk officers this meant waiting till a potentially recipient Government sent in a request. They had not been

trained to take initiatives and when requests from Governments failed to materialise they blamed that Government. It took time to get desk officers to agree that we had to visit the countries being considered for aid, explain to them what was on offer and ensure that, when a request reached us, it was something the UK could supply and it was likely to have a developmental impact.

Gradually the need to take initiatives was accepted but at first professional advisers was often sent out one at a time, and it was difficult to ensure that other professionals or administrators, who usually needed to be involved, were fully aware of the problems. Consequently huge delays and disputes took place. When I looked at some of the country programmes, I found that strings of advisers had been out separately to a country and nothing was resolved. It was clear that what was needed was for a team to go out who had the knowledge and the power to agree a project or programme on the spot.

Gradually what had seemed to many administrators as an expensive luxury - the idea of multi-disciplinary team missions to countries was accepted and resulted in much better aid programmes.

LATIN AMERICA

But back to Latin America. Shortly after my arrival Dudley Seers called me in and asked whether I would stand in for him at an International

Planned Parenthood Federation Conference in Santiago, Chile. The IPPF was big in those days and all the international great and good were associated with this important endeavour. The more I realised what was involved the more alarmed I became. It was to be opened by the President of Chile, the British Representative was to be Lord Caradon, the UK Minister Representative at the United Nations, and there were to be hundreds of attendees. Dudley was to have been the second speaker at the opening session.

"Has he taken leave of his senses?" I thought. I don't know anything about population and the economics of family planning. The only public speaking I had ever done was at a disastrous talk I had given on the "Economics of pig farming" to European farmers in Southern Rhodesia, most of whom had fallen asleep. But maybe he had identified some golden hidden qualities which I was not aware of? After all he had selected me for my present job. It was when I had agreed that the awfulness of my assignment dawned upon me. Why me? To this day his choice baffles me.

However, there was nothing for it. I had to write a twenty- minute presentation. Dudley was at his academic best as he corrected my scattered thoughts and approved them except that he did not think that I should end up being so certain that population increase was all that serious a problem. Once again I could scarcely believe my ears. Was he suggesting that I should go all the way to Chile and stand up before a high-powered, ardent population- control audience and say that, as an economist, I was not certain population increase was too great? He was. Well this was once when I intended to ignore his advice, but to spare his feelings, as he was a very nice chap and my boss into the bargain, I decided not to upset him by telling him I intended to change the ending and agree with the objectives of the conference.

The thought of having to address such a huge, prestigious conference, was a traumatic period of my life but mercifully when the great day came a semi- paralysis overcame me, as when David Livingston was being eaten by a lion, and I was able to deliver the speech as if I had not been there. I have no idea whether there was applause or not – I expect not as it sounded a rather boring speech.

Back at the Ministry, I was asked if I would mind transferring to deal with Africa, as a more junior economist had been recruited whose only experience was in Latin America. Rather reluctantly I agreed, for while Latin America was a more interesting continent, Africa was a more challenging area and one I knew well.

Over the next few years I was involved in Missions to Uganda, Kenya, Tanzania, Ethiopia, Malta, Gibraltar, Nigeria and Sierra Leone. During this period, the 1970s, we were starting to face problems which made aid disbursement increasingly difficult. There were several reasons for this. The first was the huge increase in aid and the number of donors. The World Bank, the European Community, many new country donors, were all piling in trying to meet a dreamed up target of 0.7% of their GNP as their aid contribution.

A second problem was that aid donors were not satisfied that "trickle down was working" and believed that not enough economic progress was reaching the poor. Although there was no evidence for this claim, there was a huge noble push, therefore, to help the poor more directly, mainly through rural development projects. These required new or modernised institutional and administrative structures to divert aid to the poor, but these structures and their personnel could not cope with this new emphasis.

Thirdly, there were not as many countries needing aid as there had been in the 1960s as Arab and other oil producing countries became wealthier.

Fourthly, many countries, mainly ex- colonies, became less efficient as political corruption and chaos enveloped them and aid became more difficult to disburse.

Finally, many of the "easier" traditional types of projects which Governments could manage reasonably well, had been undertaken – roads, power stations, schools and more complex multi- purpose schemes particularly which came under the heading of Rural Development, were pushed upon countries which did not have the capacity to implement complex schemes.

As a result of the first oil crises in the mid 1970s many countries faced serious balance of payments crises and we recommended that more aid should be diverted towards funding import requirements rather than projects. This was in one sense a convenient way of disbursing the aid funds available rapidly, but it was very difficult, if not impossible, to ensure that they were used as intended. Indeed, being unaccountable, politicians and key civil servants in recipient countries could and did take rake- offs from the importers who were allocated import quotas.

After working on African problems for some six years I found an opportunity to change to a different area of the world.

BACK IN GUILDFORD

Overlooking the town, as we did from our house, we were very conscious of its beautiful attractive medieval heritage and in particular its roofscape. This was under great threat from modern insensitive development proposals and as a result both Jean and I started to take an interest in its preservation.

I was intrigued to read in the local press that a very well- known consulting company had prepared a parking plan for the town. The same company had issued a report for us at the Ministry on a scheme we were being asked to fund in Ethiopia. I had to assess the report and found it of such poor quality that I decided to investigate the study they had made in Guildford. I was able to borrow a copy and discovered to my horror that they were recommending seven multi-storey car parks to be built round the town centre. Reading the report revealed that their justification was based on "need" and that they had ignored any parking fees, i.e. parking would be free. If parking were to be free the demand would, of course, be unlimited. And who would fund a huge investment which had no revenue flow? Although the report had been passed by the Council it still had to be approved by an Inspector so I sent my criticisms to him. The report was rejected.

Intrigued by another engineering consultant's report which had been accepted by the Council on a scheme to protect the town centre from serious flooding (the town had been swamped in 1968), I was able to secure a copy of this report and showed it to an engineer colleague who spotted that the engineering works proposed would mean the wholesale destruction of all the trees which were one of the finest feature of the river. And a huge embankment would make a visual dam of the beautiful upstream view. There was no justification for such destructive works since the possibility of a repeat flooding was remote, so we started a campaign to oppose the flood prevention scheme. This culminated in a public meeting which 150 people attended and we persuaded them to ask the Council to reconsider it. In view of the hostile, and indeed justified objections, the scheme was abandoned.

Clearly the town centre needed more effective interest to be paid to its preservation, so together with like-minded colleagues we decided to resuscitate the local Civic Society and I became its Chairman in 1972. We had plenty of really high powered experts available to assist us and we were able to protect several listed buildings from being demolished and get many schemes altered or rejected.

Our objections were not all that popular with developers and one day a bowler-hatted visitor knocked on my door and presented me with a charge of libel. I had written in the local newspaper that the development company who had applied to build a large shopping complex were in financial trouble, information which I had obtained from the Financial Times. Although there was no legal justification for their case, the editor and I cooked up a hasty apology as the costs of fighting them in the courts was not worth it.

After several years of successful harassment by the Civic Society, the Council decided to set up a proper Planning and Conservation Department and employ some competent staff. From then on we were able to engage in much more constructive debates with Officers and the Council.

Meanwhile, Jean had not been inactive. She decided that what the neighbourhood needed was a residents' group, partly for social reasons (none of our neighbours had welcomed us when we arrived), and partly to protect the town centre and residential areas from insensitive developments.

I tried to persuade her that she was wasting her time as the area which we lived in was not socially homogeneous. Part was a Council housing area, others middle class, and there were some really expensive houses.

However, she persisted and insisted on printing an invitation to attend a public meeting to discuss the idea of setting up an amenity group. She forced me to accompany her delivering the notice of the meeting all round the area and told me I would have to Chair the meeting.

When the great night came I was amazed to find that eighty people had turned up in the local Quaker Hall. I had to address the meeting which was attended by quite a number of articulate and very professional people who made sensible proposals to set up a working group, committees, etc.

I quickly handed over the Chair to a well-known local author and left Jean to pursue her objective. I was proved wrong, for the group has prospered and quickly built up to a membership of 700 houses, with road representatives and committees dealing with planning and social affairs. Over the last thirty years it has organised social events, dog races, Halloween parties, sunflower and pumpkin competitions, coffee mornings, boat rides, theatre visits and equally importantly, it has kept a critical eye on planning applications. My scepticism about the need for such a group has been proven to be a mistake.

Chapter Six

HOW I MET THE KING OF TONGA

PACIFIC PARADISE

One of the post-war publishing successes was "A Pattern of Islands". It was a charmingly written evocation of 22 years spent before and after the First World War in the remote Gilbert and Ellice Islands. This account of life in one of the most isolated of British Protectorates in the Pacific was written by Arthur Grimble who had served there for most of his working life as a Colonial Administrator. His description of these peaceful, sunny, coconut-covered islands, some barely 200 yards wide, where the natives could call dolphins, where huge octopuses might devour careless swimmers, was a huge success. It was a tremendously popular in the drab post-war years and generated an interest in this remote area which had just emerged from many of the appalling battles of the war between heroic American Marines and suicidal Japanese soldiers.

The Pacific had also been drawn to Britain's attention by the unexpected appearance of the huge, larger than life, Queen Salote of Tonga who joined in the procession of the Queen's coronation in 1952. Accompanied by an unusually small and unknown Tongan Foreign Minister, in her open carriage, some unkind newspaper columnists, recalling Tongans nineteenth century culinary habits, headlined him as "her lunch".

These, and such colourful American Films as "South Pacific", lent a romantic aura to this remote part of the world.

I was scheduled to lead a mission to the exotic and, then little visited, islands, of the Seychelles, when my colleague who was advising on Britain's aid programme to the Pacific told me he was resigning. He had decided to return to his Professorial Chair in Hawaii, which he had given up, inexplicably to my way of thinking, in order to join us.

During his tenure of this post he had told me that he was writing a book on the Pacific, which impressed me no end, but I was surprised that he had the time to do so. But it was not for me to judge how my colleague spent his time for I rather envied him. It seemed an odd priority for a post whose function it was to bring aid and enlightenment to those distant islands.

His decision to leave left a vacancy which, it occurred to me, could be worse filled than by me. It would mean sacrificing a long-anticipated mission to the "Eden of the Indian ocean", the Seychelles; but on the other hand the Pacific sounded as if there were many more Seychelles-like places to visit, better said to aid. It was not all that difficult to persuade my boss, who seldom got a chance to go overseas, and certainly not to places like the Seychelles, that he could take over my Seychelles mission, and to suggest a colleague to replace me on Africa. He thought my suggestion a splendid one.

It was thus that in February 1969 I became Her Majesty's Senior Economic Adviser on aid programmes to the British Dependencies in the Pacific.

AN IMPERIAL BACKWATER

There was very little left of the Empire by 1970, except for the Pacific Dependencies and a few scattered tiny remnants, too difficult to dispose of, in other parts of the world. It was an all but forgotten Imperial backwater; anyone wanting to savour the age old glory of the Imperial Administration had only to visit the Pacific.

There had been no great national interests at stake for Britain in acquiring these specks of land in the Pacific. No minerals, no strategically vital bases, and having blown up Christmas Island with our first atomic bomb this wasteful method of testing had been abandoned. It was, as a result, difficult to understand in a world which often sees naked self-interest as the only motivating factor in international acquisitions, why Britain had acquired these remote responsibilities.

However, in the nineteenth century, British explorers, missionaries and traders were scouring the world and a large Royal Navy had to be deployed somewhere, and as a result of pressures from these interests, Britain picked up a varied collection of colonies or protectorates (the latter leaving most responsibilities to local rulers) such as Fiji, Tonga, the Gilbert and Ellice Islands, the Solomon Islands and a part share (with France) in the New Hebrides.

Missionaries, who were keen to convert heathens and suppress slavery and cannibalism, played a vital role in the development of these territories. While many criticise their suppression of traditional cultures it should be borne in mind that these included pretty continuous warfare, cannibalism, polygamy and infanticide. The missionaries played a key role in ending many of these practices. They were also active in securing the suppression of slavery, in mitigating the excesses of indentured labour, and they often protected the interests of naive local people by acting as effective intermediaries between them and rapacious traders.

With a large, underemployed Royal Navy, the British administration was able to absorb new colonies quite easily, especially since the Treasury insisted that they must be financially self-supporting. This meant that the people who "joined" the Empire had to raise the taxes to pay for their colonial administrators. This latter requirement was largely fulfilled, but it meant that there was very little money available for the development of them, until aid programmes started in the post-war world. The Administration concentrated on maintaining law and order, something they did very effectively.

The islands had been populated thousands of years ago from the Asian mainland through quite incredible sea-going migrations. These had led to a good deal of cultural and physical diversity. Curiously those closest to the mainland, the Melanesians of the Solomon Islands, New Hebrides and the southern Gilberts, were least developed and their people were much smaller in stature and far more backward culturally and economically than those further East and North, the Polynesians. The Polynesians of Fiji, Tonga, Samoa and the French dependencies around Tahiti, were and are, strong self confident people. Heavier rainfall and more fertile islands in the east were without doubt a major factor accounting for this difference, though only the strongest could have survived the incredible sea journeys which these long migrations required.

Fiji, the largest of the dependencies, was also the richest. However, much of this wealth resulted from migrant Indian sugar workers who had been introduced by the British, as local workers, quite understandably, did not think that working in sugar plantations was worthwhile. The Indians, like all immigrants, had been exceptionally industrious and had become economically successful and were almost as numerous as the native Fijians. Since there was no cultural adaptation by the Indians an understandable tension existed between these two cultures.

The Tongans had developed a sophisticated power structure based upon a Monarchy complete with Nobles. Since all Pacific societies were accustomed to the idea of Chiefs, this was not as alien a system as might be supposed.

The Gilbert and Ellice Islands on the other hand, like the Solomons, were very much a British administrative convenience which did not entirely relate to the cultural and economic situation of these diverse and distant poorer, backward islands. They were culturally and economically much less developed than the Polynesians to the east.

The Condominium of the New Hebrides was a most curious colonial Anglo-French hybrid. The French had colonised the nearby Territory of New Caledonia, which produced 40% of the world's supply of nickel, and as a result they took an interest in adjoining territories where constitutional changes might threaten or affect this precious prize. It was agreed to have a joint administration with Britain of the nearby New Hebrides, which meant however that there were three Administrations: a British Administration, a French Administration and a joint Condominium Administration. There were two education and two health systems which were responsible to the individual administrations, but Police, Customs and Excise were a joint responsibility. There were three Finance Departments, English, French and Condominium. It is difficult to envisage a more complex and absurd way of running a country.

This was the "Parish" on whose economic future I had to advise. It was not exactly a large one (my responsibilities also covered other dependencies such as Gibraltar, the Falklands and the Caribbean Islands), but it was distant and it was enormously exciting to think I was going to be paid to visit these islands in warm coconut climates with their colourful coral lagoons.

TAKING OVER

After a few days at my new desk I was surprised to have no visits from the floor messenger who was responsible for distributing files to staff for them to "action". Normally, in other departments, one's in-tray was piled with files and reports with requests from administrators, who were responsible for country aid programmes, for advice.

After a week of inaction I thought I had better go and find out what the Administrators responsible for the Pacific were up to. The response I got took me aback for I was told "Almost all our requests for aid are under £20,000 and we do not really need any economic advice as the amounts are too small to bother you."

I realised why my predecessor had been able to write a book. For two years he had happily accepted this assessment of his role and being an academic, quite easily adjusted to it.

Of course it was true that the economic appraisal of small one-off requests for aid for worthy infrastructure projects such as roads, water supplies, agriculture, health and administration, which were parts of ongoing activities, was not practicable. However, we were spending several million pounds a year on these islands and we needed to be clear what we were achieving and whether this aid was being used to generate further development.

What was our economic strategy? Had we any policies for the area? These islands with small populations could easily be overwhelmed with aid and become aid dependent. So what were our objectives? The administrators did not know. As far as they were concerned their job, since they were relatively junior, was to meet the demands from the Governors of these tiny territories. It was not for them to question whether the requests were justified.

It seemed to me pretty odd that this situation had been going on for years without anyone questioning it. I therefore went to speak to the Assistant Secretary, the Head of Department. He was a very lively likeable fellow who had been pushed out of the Foreign Office to its subordinate Overseas Development Administration (as it had been renamed) as he had dared to challenge the need for the Navy to refit its expensive aircraft carriers. He readily appreciated that we really should have an overview of what our aid was achieving and what it should achieve. He also agreed that this could only be obtained by a tour of these Territories by his Senior Economic Adviser and an administrator, unfortunately not himself, but his operational subordinate.

I was surprised to discover that my predecessor had never been on any Missions and that this was the first one the Ministry would send. I was asked by the Assistant Secretary to tread carefully as Colonial Governors and Administrators were unaccustomed to visits by such curious professionals as economists, and the administrator who was to come with me was too junior to overawe those we would meet.

I had been surprised, and indeed pleased and relieved when I joined the Ministry that the financially beleaguered British Government allowed us to travel first class. This was not as lavish as it is today but one did have comfortable spacious seats with choices of caviar, lobster or salmon as hors d'oeuvres (attractive hostesses were delighted to serve all three if requested), a choice of beef or lamb off the bone served with silver cutlery, and huge colourful menus accompanied with an envelope which encouraged one to post (free) to anyone one wanted to annoy or impress, as well as as much drink as requested.

In view of the immense amount of travel one had to do during the year, especially flying out to the Pacific, this was not an unreasonable staff perquisite.

During the course of the next two years I made four trips to the Pacific, initially to secure an overall view of the Islands, which much to my surprise the World Bank claimed in their statistics were amongst the poorest countries in the world, and later to investigate specific projects and problems. The conclusions I reached about them were not ones I had expected.

THE CONDOMINIUM OF THE NEW HEBRIDES

My first tour was made via New Caledonia, a French Territory, which I had to transit through for a day as there was no direct air link to the New Hebrides. My first destination was a shock. Noumea, its capital, was a glittering mass of concrete and glass skyscrapers with, outside it, the largest industrial complex, processing its nickel, I had ever seen. The town was full of elegant, expensively dressed, French residents sitting in splendid cafes or in luxury hotels. This was not the coconut, lagoon-lined Pacific I had expected. There were not all that many local people either. Most were French. And much of the land had been taken over by French farmers so that it had become very much part of France. The reason? Nickel! 40% of the world's nickel came from this tiny island and the French Government had it firmly in its grasp. Even the President of France was reputed to have shares in the nickel operation.

However, that was a French problem not a British one.

It was only a short hop over to the hybrid dependency of the New Hebrides. This was another world. Vila, the capital, was a small run-down place; a few streets with a few Indian and Chinese traders. Most of the local population lived in close-to-stone-age conditions in heavily forested rural areas. There were two secondary schools, French and English, two hospitals, French and English, and a few miles of roads.

The British Resident, a charming fellow, nicely dressed in white shorts with long white stockings (but alas no pith helmet), lived in a comfortable bungalow on an island just off the coast, safe from the one time spear throwing unfriendly local people.

The local people had developed some unique and interesting customs, one of which the rest of the world has picked up. This was "bungee jumping". It was not known by this name at that time but it was developed by the natives on Tanna Island.

The natives of Tanna had, as a ritual, developed the custom of once a year requiring their male adolescents to throw themselves off a 70-foot- high tree. Tied around their legs was a liana. Lianas do stretch, a bit, and their length was so well calculated that they ensured that the participant did not actually hit the ground with his head. It was so calculated that his head would just land on the soft earth they had prepared for him.

There were no records of how many times the length of the liana was miscalculated but presumably, since it was an annual ritual, the majority survived what seemed to be a suicidal custom. But some enterprising European had copied this daring bit of foolishness and from time to time one can see, in London, bored or lunatic adolescents attached to bits of elastic throwing themselves off a gigantic crane overlooking the Thames.

"Cargo cults" were another unusual feature of these remote islands. They arose because bewildered natives, seeing the huge wealth of the foreigners, and subsequently the even greater wealth of US soldiers suddenly appearing in the New Hebrides during the war thought that if they copied them they too might have access to it. Since the airfields that Americans built led to great wealth arriving in aeroplanes, they hit on the idea of building airstrips – and waiting for "manna" to arrive. Seeing Americans speaking into telephones, and listening to radios, they built wooden models and hoped that this would bring in the "goodies". This they had seen occur with American soldiers, so why should they not muscle in on this heaven-sent bonanza of aeroplanes landing loaded with beer and Hershie bars? So these cults prospered. It was said that an aircraft landed on one of their strips once, but this is rumour.

Many would say that there was really not much difference between these cults and many more sophisticated religions in the world: these were just a little less sophisticated and but more direct in their prayers.

The New Hebrides was a curious amalgamation of a stone age culture with French, Indian and Chinese commercialism, (it even included a brothel whose Madam so I was told by the District Officer was well received by society), and a British Administration straight out of a Victorian Boy Scout story. Its bizarre cocktail of cultures made it quite unique in the world.

British Administrators, all neatly clad in white shorts and long stockings, efficiently and politely organised a tour of the Territory's limited infrastructure.

DEVELOPMENT ISSUES

We were whisked around to assess existing and planned schools, wharfs, plantations and a hospital for which our approval and support were being sought. Most of them were sensible, quite low level schemes, which fitted well into the culture and economy. I only had problems with one project, that of a "prestige hospital to compete with the French." With the amount of land available, the proposed two storey hospital, requiring lifts, seemed to me to be an unnecessary luxury and the problems of servicing lifts in this tiny territory seemed to have been overlooked, so I said it was not our function to use aid funds to "outdo the French".

This upset the British Resident no end as he was not used to his wishes being challenged, so we agreed that I would discuss it with our Chief Medical Adviser on my return to England. I did this and was turned on by the Chief Medical Officer who was clearly unused to being thwarted and went purple with fury and made the extraordinary threat that "if I opposed his project he would hit me over the head with an axe". Never in a career filled with challenges to pet schemes had such a violent and bizarre response arisen. Fortunately no such weapon was to hand and when he calmed down we agreed a compromise on a one- storey "luxury" hospital.

The provision of improved education and of better health were the top priorities together with agricultural improvements, but the lack of technical and administrative skills could only be remedied by imports of expatriate technical assistance. It was all too easy to overwhelm this tiny country with expensive experts and administrators which would lead to a dependency culture. This was not what our "Development" Policy was about. Too much aid was a real danger especially as there were those who wished to compete with the French and for good or bad reasons ensure a pro-British client. While the New Hebrideans would have been be delighted to have aid showered upon them it would have make them financially even more dependent on the metropolitan powers.

GILBERT AND ELLICE ISLANDS

"It was clear daylight six feet down in the limpid water – the brute's eyes burned at me as I turned towards his cranny – that was the last thing I saw as I blacked out and rose into his clutches as I covered my eyes from its tentacles. Something whipped round my forearm and the back of my neck – another something slapped itself high on my forehead, I felt it crawling inside my singlet. My boyhood nightmare was upon me – I felt the constriction of those disgusting arms, a mouth began to nuzzle below my throat – I gave a kick, rose to the surface and turned on my back, the brute sticking to my chest like a tumour. My mouth was covered by some flabby horror."

This was Arthur Grimble's amazing account of using his body as bait to attract an octopus from its lair in one of the lagoons in the Gilbert and Ellice Islands. Why did he do it? He stumbled across two lads who were fishing for octopuses and they dared him to copy them. What else could a chap do? A District Commissioner scared of an octopus? Never!

When he surfaced the two young lads pounced on the octopus and bit it between the eyes and the horror was over.

It is difficult to imagine anything so awful as being enveloped by an octopus, especially since it was voluntarily carried out to show local youngsters that the District Officer was perfectly capable of doing what they did, but it is one of the many tales of derring-do which this lone representative of His Majesty's Colonial Service felt it was his duty to perform.

His two books are packed full of Boys' Own Adventures; calling porpoises, arresting homicidally jealous husbands, sailing dangerous oceans on a tiny outrigger, fighting sharks, putting down revolts, all of which occurred during the many years he spent on these delicate slips of coral in the Pacific Ocean.

The Gilbert and Ellice Islands, named after some of their earlier British "discoverers", consist of 33 islands spread over 2000 miles and with a population of around 100,000 people. The islands, thanks to palms, fish and pandannus (a local tree crop), despite poor soils provided a reasonable if monotonous subsistence living for the inhabitants. Fresh water was the greatest problem.

Grimble's two books, and a wealth of notes about customs and history, are not only an entrancing account of a lonely European life spent in a very different culture (at one stage he was separated from his wife and 4 children for 7 years), but it is a scholarly and unique story of Gilbertese life which will stand for all time.

He seeks to establish from innumerable discussions on all the islands the history of the people who travelled these vast oceans. Their outrigger canoes, which developed from Chinese sailing techniques, enabled them to sail to windward, to the mysterious east, and took them as far as New Zealand and to the even more remote Easter Island. More tantalisingly Grimble believes they even reached South America, "a land called Maiwa - the wall at the side of the world, four moons sail to eastward, a land that stretches to the north without end and to the south without end – beyond the furthest eastward island it lays – a wall of mountains up against the place where the sun rises." Did they really see the Andes?

Interspersed in the histories and legends there is interwoven within it a profound interest and respect for those he has arbitrarily been chosen to rule and his tribute to them could not be better set out than in his own elegant sincere prose:

"The islands I had chosen blindly, for the reason that they were romantically remote was peopled by a race who, despite the old savagery of their wars, and the grimness of their endless battle with the sea, was princes in laughter and friendship, poetry and love."

Could any people expect a better and more beautiful compliment?

The Gilbert and Ellice Islands were formally declared a Protectorate when HMS Royalist appeared in 1892 and flew the British flag for the first time. The islands and groups within them had hitherto been engaged in endless feuds and wars and the advent of this powerful weapon of war miraculously brought these to an end. "Pax Britannica" had real meaning in these distant, hitherto warring, islands.

Grimble recalls how a very old woman told him, " up to the coming of the Flag" – when she must have been about 70, they had never known what it was, as maid or wife, to stray outside the village settlement of her menfolk – "In those days" she said "death was on the right hand and on the left. If we wandered north, we were killed or raped. If we went south, we were killed or raped. If we returned alive from walking abroad we were killed by our husbands who said we had gone forth seeking to be raped. Yet how beautiful life is our villages now that there is no killing and war no more"

Seldom can there have been such an eloquent testimony to imperial rule.

Yet imperial rule was scarcely evident. There were just a handful of administrators paid mean, meagre salaries from taxes collected from the inhabitants. Yet they ruled over thousands of consenting and previously warring adults. Admittedly the possibility of a visit by a gunboat would have been at the back of the minds of those who had anti-social pretensions, but basically the Administration went with the social grain, used existing systems of justice and control, (other than when murders took place) and respected the values and behaviour of the people. Grimble and the few colleagues he had were able to maintain law and order in a way that had not been possible before.

The missionaries, however, played an important role in developing, through education and worship, new opportunities and new gods which rapidly, if superficially, took hold. Slavery and cannibalism, both of which were rife, were effectively abolished and missionaries often acted as effective intermediaries between exploiting traders and naive natives. Missionary activity was not always welcome; they abolished ancestor worship, insisted on more European ways of dressing and persuaded the Government to abolish polygamy (despite opposition from the Colonial Administration). However, on balance, the missionary role should be seen as a positive interference in a society which, while having many virtues, also had many gruesome ones. Anyhow, as Grimble records, as with all Christian conversions many old pagan habits discreetly continued.

What clearly emerges from Grimble's book is the spirit of public service, which he and his colleagues saw as their duty to the people over whom they ruled. Not many other imperial powers and not many rulers in other poor independent countries of the world could legitimately make this claim.

DEVELOPMENT

I was happy to note that the tiny 14-seater aircraft which was to carry us from Fiji to the Gilbert and Ellice Islands was powered by 4 propeller engines, 1 for every 3.5 passengers; must have been very costly to fly, I thought.

After some 4 hours the Ellice Islands came into view. They were set in sparkling clear blue lagoons with ubiquitous coconut trees shading pure white beaches. They were just as attractive as all the tourist brochures claimed. The airstrip at Funafuti, the capital of this sub-group of islands with only about 10,000 inhabitants, was flattened coral and the terminal was a simple open thatched- roofed building. It adjoined the the small town, better said village, and which was about 50 yards away, which consisted of a couple of shops and a hotel with 5 bedrooms. More alluring was the nearby lagoon which was so tempting. This looked too good to be true and while the pilot was away I quickly changed into my swimming trunks and went for a swim. It is difficult to describe the contentment one felt from this exotic swim which was not affected by a slightly irritated pilot who came in search of a missing passenger.

As we flew off I could envisage a plethora of requests for aid for an air terminal, a new landing strip and all sorts of navigational landing aids from the airline using it; and a new hotel.

Another few hours and Tarawa, also a feast of sapphire lagoons and golden sands, appeared on the horizon. The main "islands" were three-quarters of the way round a huge lagoon and were amazingly narrow, maybe 200 yards wide but some 35 miles long. There were no hills or features to this delicate structure and one wondered how it survived the turbulent waves of the Pacific? It was rather disconcerting to think that we were only a few feet above sea level and that the massive waves which thundered day and night against the reef could easily sweep everyone away. The reason why they did not, so I was assured, was that the islands are the coral encrusted peaks of huge mountains and the surrounding sea so deep that devastating waves do not occur.

One hoped this was right. However, should the sea level rise more than 10 feet these islands would disappear.

The fragile "International Terminal", consisting of a building with a thatched roof without walls, was in danger of being blown away if the aircraft engines on takeoff were too near.

We were housed in the only hotel, a pleasant ten- roomed building, with a large open veranda overlooking an enticingly clear lagoon. One could hear, from almost any location on the island, the dramatic roar of the Pacific waves as they pounded the protective encircling reef.

One was struck by the cleanliness of the island, the pleasantness of a good- looking people and their simple dress which was basically a sarong for women and a long loin cloth for men.

The houses were simple thatched buildings raised from the ground and open at the sides to catch every possible cool breeze. Privacy was at a premium as all activity, unless the straw mat walls were unrolled, was subject to public view.

The administrators, in their usual neat colonial garb, showed us around their modest infrastructure. A school, hospital, coconut plantations, all managed by a few tens of expatriate administrators. Considerable efforts were being made to expand and improve the educational system as it was obvious that the demands for independence were growing, and there was no wish by Britain to stand in the way.

However, there were no Gilbertese whose education extended beyond secondary level, a qualification which might have been more than sufficient in earlier days but was hardly adequate in the modern world which independent rulers would have to deal with.

We were invited for supper by the Chief Elected Member who was being groomed as President or Prime Minister. His house, most unusually, was partially concrete but with a thatched roof, the sitting room was carpeted with palm mats, decorated on the walls by family photographs and a proud secondary- school leaving certificate. There were only two comfortable chairs in the sitting room so he had to sit on a hard chair to entertain us. Hardly an extravagant ambience for a future chief. We discussed Gilberts history; "the old men" could recite back to 50 generations, and somewhat to my surprise discovered that Samoans from the East had swept over the islands some 400 years ago, as I had assumed all migration was from Asia in the West. This explained the somewhat sturdier physiques of the Gilberts as compared with Solomon Islanders and New Hebrideans. He had no complaints about the Missionaries or the Administration, which he could have made as we were on our own.

Possibly to get us out of the way, we had a two day tour of a neighbouring island – another incredibly long and narrow coconut growing strip of land. As we walked through the coconut groves (there was no road), the Pacific roaring in the distance, we were amazed to see stretching high above the coconut palms the steeple of a church. It was about four stories high and had been built in 1904 by the locals under the guidance of a missionary. It seemed quite incongruous and must have been to the locals what a Gothic Cathedral would have been to medieval peasants in northern Europe. One reflected whether a small community capable of this achievement with minimal outside guidance really needed much aid.

We also visited the District Officer's residence, a large thatched construction consisting of two rooms, bamboo walls and floors of palm thatch. The shower was water can. While delightfully picturesque, with a view over the lagoon which tourists would pay a fortune for, one could not but reflect on the mental resilience which a British District Officer would have to possess to serve for months if not years, in such a restricted environment. Maybe it was a good thing the Colonial Service rejected me. I could not imagine myself spending long alone in these conditions.

We were impressed by the generally efficient way the Protectorate was administered, but it was essentially geared to the maintenance of law and order and provision of health and education services. The economy was very dependent financially on income from phosphates from one of its distant islands and these were due to run out in a decade. There were very few other local resources which could make up this loss but an innovative scheme for training young men as sailors was being started. It entailed educating them on land on what they would have to do on a modern ship, and then flying them out to join a tanker anywhere in the world. The Gilberts adapted well and their earnings and remittances home would provide a valuable source of new income.

However, with the large amount of aid available the danger was that a lack of local skills would be filled by expensive expatriates. This meant new, expensive, housing and the society and economy could become top heavy. There was also the underlying problem of a rapid population increase which needed urgent attention through family planning. There were no other indigenous resources of consequence to sustain a much larger population.

We were quickly able to draw up a modest investment programme in which we prioritised family planning, education and health.

THE KINGDOM OF TONGA

This was quite a shock. All the authoritative international statistics indicated that Tonga was one of the poorest countries in the world. The tiny aircraft glided down, the pilot kindly letting me sit in the co-pilot's seat, onto a soft, grass, runway surrounded by a tropical affluence of trees. We could see as we had flown in, an island of gay green forest cover surrounded by bright blue lagoons; no shortage of rain in Tonga and plenty of responsively fertile soils.

As we drove into the capital the roadside was verdant and alive with flowers, red hibiscuses predominating. There were trees loaded with coconuts and bananas, and all houses were on tidy neatly cultivated, 8.25 acre plots, to which every family was entitled, and which they scrupulously maintained with mower- cut lawns and with masses of bold coloured flowers.

Accustomed to so many countries with slums surrounding their main cities this was a delightful and quite unique change. These people "the poorest in the world"? Surely not.

We drove into the charmingly softly named capital, Nuku'alofa. It was beautifully tidy, and the wide traffic- free roads were lined by wooden sidewalks and rows of well maintained wooden houses and shops with colourful pitched roofs. Just off the centre, larger houses were set in ample lawns with flowering gardens.

There was a splendid wooden Gothic- style cathedral, with white towers and a cheerful red roof. There was a palace as well; a large well maintained Edwardian style building, with generous verandas, painted an immaculate white with lots of turrets and also with a bright red roof. This was the most attractive capital of any of the many small countries I had been fortunate enough to visit.

With a population of around 100,000 spread over some 34 islands, but mainly concentrated in two, Tonga had voluntarily become a British Protectorate in 1900. British involvement in the administration of the country was minimal as there existed a Monarchy which was capable of managing its own affairs. Britain was represented by an able Consul General who acted as required as adviser and a link between the two countries.

The natural wealth of the islands both on land and sea showed itself in the size and nature of the average Tongan – large and relaxed and oozing self-confidence. Originally bored, testosterone fuelled young males had set out to improve their cuisine through raids on other islands, but mssionaries and the British had converted them to less aggressive ways of gastronomy and towards socially more constructive activities such a church- going and rugby. The Christian Church had taken firm root and banished many of the easy going practices of the past for a sterner evangelical life. Sunday was a day of rest and even the Scots would have balked at not being allowed to swim on that day.

At the turn of the century, a clergyman, John Baker, had been a powerful influence over the Monarchy but at the same time acted very successfully on behalf of the Tongans in dealing with ruthless trading companies.

The King was a benign absolute ruler, appointing most his Cabinet who were usually selected from a list of 40 Nobles who were sort of feudal barons. The system was charmingly archaic, but did not appear oppressive or particularly authoritarian, and was well accepted. However, one wondered if it would survive and adapt to the changing social aspirations of those emerging from the expanding educational system.

The following day we had an audience with the King in his splendid wooden Palace. He was sitting in a middle- sized drawing room on an Edwardian settee in a room crowded with photographs of his ancestors, with Victorian furniture scattered informally around.

He was a large man, as befitting a son of Queen Salote and a product of such a rich environment, weighing probably 20 stone. He was dressed in a simple, long, grey toga down to his sandaled feet, and round his ample waist he had wrapped a huge straw mat which was a sign of the Tongan nobility.

He wore dark glasses and spoke with a clear but high voice in perfect English. I struck a lucky conversational vein when I asked him if he had read "Sharp's Ancient Voyagers in the Pacific", which he had and he explained to me how navigators were able to embark on such long journeys. Navigators followed birds, which could fly as far as 500 miles from land and return to it at night. They could tell from cloud formations and reflected light in the sky from white sandy beaches if there was land in the distance. They could tell from the flotsam in the sea, from the colour of the water and even from smell, where they were. He gave me a useful tip. If short of fresh water at sea fish heads contained some which one could drink. From there we went on to discuss primitive family planning. When populations seemed to be getting excessive, abortions, infanticide and exile were the agreed solutions. From this interesting debate we then went on to discuss some of the latest books: "The Naked Ape", "The Territorial Imperative", and "Gang Warfare"; the role of trade unions, crime, decimalisation, social structures and right- hand driving. We had some two hours of splendid discussion and when I came away my republican principles were badly dented.

We then went on to meet the Cabinet. This consisted of the Prime Minister, who was the King's younger brother, two Governors of neighbouring islands, the Minister of Finance (ex- London School of Economics), the Minister of Police, a Minister without Portfolio (degrees Harvard, Cambridge and Auckland) and Joe, the Minister of Lands and Education. Delegation of responsibility was virtually unknown and we were told that the Cabinet spent an entire afternoon discussing whether a civil servant was entitled to import a refrigerator; it was thought he had imported one the previous year, but it might have been sold to a relative. Very strict Sunday observance laws existed. No picking of coconuts, no swimming, no games and no exchange of money and this led to an urgent Cabinet meeting to determine whether an international flight which had been delayed by a day could fly in on a Sunday.

We were invited to several Tongan meals, better described as open-air banquets, in which the amount of food available and eaten was enormous. One stands out as it was a nineteenth- birthday party and some sixty hefty Tongans were invited. The table which must have been about forty- feet long, consisted of seventeen suckling pigs, thirty chickens, six huge ,whole, cooked and raw fish, roast lamb, curried lamb, prawns, crayfish, bully beef, taro, water melon, and paw paw with jelly and ice cream. The table was loaded to about a foot high with food which one picked out and carried away on fresh palm leaves.

DEVELOPMENT

If one took into account the fact that Tongans had more food than they could eat, that they did not have to spend money as we do keeping warm, that they had virtually no transport costs, and self-build housing, they were certainly not the poorest country in the world. Arguably they could be classified amongst the richest.

There had been an aid programme which mainly consisted of the provision of an inter-island ferry, a new wharf, improved airport facilities and some modest help with education. All were performing well. There really was no great need for increases in aid, and with other donors lining up, a reduction would be perfectly reasonable.

Clearly, with an increasing population and much of the land being already allocated, the problems, which could challenge not only the country's natural resources but its social system, could be considerable. Family planning and some form of constitutional improvements seemed high priorities.

It occurred to me that if there was a post going for an Economic Adviser on my retirement I might put in for it.

FIJI

"Don't worry too much Gordon" said my amiable Fijian dinner host "if the missionaries had not come we could have been eating you for dinner tonight." This splendidly amusing put-down by my host had been in response to my injudicious argument about the adverse impact of missionaries on Pacific cultures.

Of the many countries and cultures I have had the good fortune to visit, I have seldom come across a people with whom one could be totally relaxed. The Fijians had no hang-ups about British rule, no inferiority complex, and possessed a good natured self-confidence which was relaxing and refreshing. The fact that this very senior civil servant could deal with what many would regard as a rather sensitive issue speaks for itself.

With a population nearing a million, nearly half of Indian origin who had been brought in to establish a thriving sugar industry at the turn of the century, and plenty of tropical rainfall, Fiji was Britain's largest colony in the Pacific. These immensely green and fertile islands created powerful Fijian rugby players who, together with the Polynesian Tongan and Samoans, have effectively challenged the world's most powerful rugby nations.

The islands had quite willingly accepted colonial status in 1870, probably because as in so many other cases, internecine warfare had reached a peak and British rule had put a welcome end to it.

Cannibalism is not widely discussed in the Pacific, politeness and political correctness no doubt account for the fact that it is not a suitable topic for social occasions. Nevertheless this custom, far more widespread than many care to admit, seems to have reached quite abnormal proportions in these otherwise idyllic islands. While attacks by bored, frustrated, testosterone- hyped youths must have accounted for many of the annual warring expeditions to neighbouring islands, no doubt population pressures also created the circumstance which led to attacks on other islands.

A more attractive feature of the culture, certainly to the first sex-starved eighteenth century European sailors who emerged unscathed from the horrors of oceanic travel, was the friendliness of so many of the local women they encountered. Captain Cook's men almost destroyed their vessels looking for nails with which to reward the ladies for a nights revels. One nail was at first quite sufficient to entice a lady on board but after a few weeks there was 100% inflation and two nails were demanded. Sexual mores, however, were not totally uninhibited, as local male possessiveness often created serious problems for wayward nail- collecting wives.

Polygamy was common and there are many stories of customs which allowed wives to lie with close relatives or friends. Grimble recounts how a man and his wife were so grateful to him for helping him that they came to him offering her to him as a mark of thanks. Grimble, while politely declining the offer, was able to extract from the wife that she was not really very keen on the idea and would have preferred a local man, but was complying with her husbands' wishes.

Women did not have all that much say in how they might make use of their natural attractions. Polygamy was standard and widely accepted by women. When at the insistence of the missionaries it was abolished, it was reported that many of the women, no longer part of their husband's "harem", committed suicide. However much it is argued that polygamy was culturally acceptable, it is difficult to believe that this was a fair situation for women or that its abolition, on balance, was not justified.

The colonial presence in Fiji was low key. There was a Colonial Governor, but the Prime Minister was a tall, large, dignified Fijian Chief, several Ministers were Fijian and so were many senior civil servants. There were no Fijian Indian civil servants at senior level and it was in the private sector, where they were able to exercise their impressive entrepreneurial skills and energy, that they predominated.

Fijian independence was coming up soon and I had several visits to agree an aid programme with them. One of the most controversial projects had been a £1m coconut subsidy programme. Fiji is a natural coconut habitat and therefore the idea of encouraging farmers to grow more coconuts was not without merit. Unfortunately the programme entailed subsidizing farmers to plant more coconuts. It was unfortunate as handing out subsidies to any farmers to do what they were already doing presents daunting problems of accountability. Nevertheless I was asked to report on its success or otherwise and the Fijian Government organised a tour for me of coconut areas.

Meeting farmers was not novel for me but I was most impressed to be received so enthusiastically at the villages I visited. Invariably there were some 50 neatly clad farmers sitting on the ground under trees or other shelter waiting for "Big fella come England". I was offered a seat, one of those canvas chairs which District Commissioners in old films about Africa sit on. I was then addressed by the Village Council Leader welcoming me and handing me, on his knees and bowing as he did it, a coconut shell containing a muddy-looking drink made from local root crops. As I drank the far from attractive contents, the assembled crowd gave a throaty roar and clapped their hands.

I only learned afterwards that I should have burped my appreciation of their drink but I was too busy thinking how I should address them. Out of the corner of my eye I spied some American tourists who had come across this marvellously imperial encounter and were busily recording it to delight their friends back in Minnesota.

I wondered whether I should say that I brought "Fraternal greetings from the workers of England" but decided that this would not go down well amongst the toiling masses in Britain who might think that handing out their taxes to Pacific Islanders was not high on their priority list. I then thought perhaps I might bring greetings from "The people of England" but I was not quite sure that this would be thought fair in England by anyone but readers of "The Guardian" and "The Times." Instead, it being Fiji where loyalty to the Crown was strong, I started by saying that I brought greetings from "Her Majesty". This went down very well. I then went on to congratulate them on their village, and their coconuts, stressing that the Queen wished to help them help themselves and therefore our aid was directed to helping them grow more coconuts. I could not help reflecting, as I saw myself in this "Sanders of the River" scene, what my boisterous fellow commuters on the 7.28 from Guildford to Waterloo would say had they seen me acting out this stereotypical colonial role.

However, it all went down well and I had the ultimate accolade from the Permanent Secretary of Finance who was accompanying me, "Gordon - you would have made an excellent District Commissioner." See what the Colonial Office missed, I thought, when they rejected me as "red".

We made visits to two of the other major islands, staying in delightful rural hotels, frequently near the sea, and making more speeches to villagers about how splendid they were and how the Queen wanted to help them to help themselves. I think the compliment about my performance may have gone to my head as I seemed to make an abnormally large number of speeches. However, all this could easily have come to an untimely end when I decided to take a nap one lazy afternoon on the grass at the edge of a quiet blue lagoon in the shade of some coconut trees. I was awoken by a thump near my head and there, lying inches away, was a coconut. Coconuts growing on palm trees are not those brown wizened things one sees at country fairs which are glued to the poles they are perched on, but massive great green lumps of vegetation weighing many pounds which would be quite fatal if bounced on one's head. This one landed inches from my right ear. I dread to think what the sub-editors of the papers might have said had it hit me: "Economist killed by coconut during coconut survey" or "Don't sleep under a coconut tree."

Mind you, it would have a saved me the embarrassment of having to advise that the coconut scheme needed to be wound up and more accountable aid projects considered.

I was able to endorse several projects but I concluded that both a new airport, and at least its landing strip, was woefully extravagant and unjustified and that the architects of a new hospital should go back and design something more appropriate to Fiji than to Britain. This did not go down too well with the spending departments but I had support from the Fiji Treasury and some modifications were eventually agreed.

Fiji was, I concluded, a well-run little country, prosperous in a real sense and it did not really need much aid; the aid we could usefully provide was essentially to improve and upgrade existing Government services. And there was no justification for providing assistance to coconut farmers for doing what they should be doing anyway.

SOLOMON ISLANDS

The view from the only hotel in the capital, Honiara, was superb. One sat on a huge tiled veranda overlooking a cool blue lagoon surrounded by white sands and green, shady, coconut palms. A perfect tourist magnet. There was only one thing wrong with it. It never changed. After half an hour of gazing at it, it was still there. And that is the real problem with the Pacific. It is a tropical paradise, (well - ignoring rains, typhoons and tsunamis) but there are no seasons in the Pacific.

Day after indolent day one had this hot, sometimes unbelievably hot, unchanging scenario and one longed for a change. There is a lot to be said for living in a temperate climate with four clear seasons per year, leaving one waiting, sometimes longing, for spring, or summer or autumn; and even winter with imagined log fires and warm comfort can be appealing. It is easy to get bored in the Pacific. In fact there is a common affliction called "coral atollitis" which afflicts many people once a year – they go slightly odd. Sometimes on the smaller islands they jump into a canoe and are never seen again; unless they hit upon an island.

The Solomon Islands were declared a Protectorate about the same time as the rest in 1870. Once again pressure came from missionaries to protect local people from slavers, to put down cannibalism and sexual licence, and in this case there was also the fact that the German Imperialists were collecting islands in the Pacific. Who knows what consequences this would have if Britain did not acquire some of this real estate.

The boundaries were set as an administrative convenience rather than to encompass a homogeneous social group of people sharing some common purpose or some common threat. As with the other Pacific territories, Britain's involvement was pretty minimal and restricted to the laudable aims of suppressing slavery, cannibalism, war and polygamy, and providing a legal framework for the Solomon Islanders to achieve this.

There was one State Secondary School, a hospital, a port and an airport, and quite a number of neatly dressed administrators to see that it was well run. Indeed it was well run though, slightly unusually, there were some young dynamic administrators who were keen to help develop the Protectorate.

Honiara, the capital, was not much more than a one-street town with a hotel, some shops and a yacht club for the Administration.

The local people still dressed in neat cool sarongs, the lush mountainous forests produced masses of beautiful flowers which decorated the houses and the Melanesians themselves, as they wore them in their hair. The standard of living was generally very low, but they lived in a fertile environment and food was ample and living in it not arduous.

Their quiet lives had been violently intruded upon in 1942 when 35,000 Japanese invaded them with the intention of disrupting the link between the USA and Australia. This led to an American counter- invasion and for nearly six months in 1942 the battle of Guadalcanal was fought here. Some 60,000 American troops with air and sea support, after some of the most vicious fighting, defeated the Japanese. The eventual casualties tell us a lot about this war: Japanese 30,000 killed, Americans 7,000 killed. The Americans lost 615 aircraft and 29 ships.

DEVELOPMENT ISSUES

The scarcity of locally trained people meant that effective provision of more aid could only be achieved by increasing the numbers of expensive expatriates, burdening an already tight budget. This would require an ever- larger annual expenditure which the economy was unlikely to sustain without aid funding, thus requiring the Aid Programme to fund annual costs, something which it had been sensibly decided we should not do.

The basic problem was that the objective of wanting rapid development could only be achieved by using far more expatriates to supervise the expansion of the meagre infrastructure, as there were few well trained local staff, but this would require heavy investment in European standard housing and an increase in the annual budget to pay salaries. It was not Government policy to fund local annual costs of this nature. Local people could and should be trained for this task but it would be many years before this could be achieved. The islands would become increasingly dependent on British Government hand-outs.

The most appropriate development policy would have been to provide more educational (and health) assistance and postpone capital aid assistance until there were enough local experts to manage their own aid programmes. Alas this was not likely to go down well with either the local administration or my administrative colleagues in London who wanted to disburse as much aid as possible.

But basic to all these issues would be how to maintain the national unity of a group of island cultures arbitrarily brought together to form a new, though small, nation state. There were no external pressures threatening the country to induce a sense of unity. Opposition to British rule would not create a sense of national unity, as it had in other countries, as British rulers were obviously anxious to abandon their responsibilities as soon as possible.

REFLECTIONS ON "PARADISE"

There is no doubt that colourful brochures of these exotic languorous islands do not deceive the tourist. The beaches are splendid, the warm sea a turquoise green-blue and even better, the underwater coral jungles with their sparkling queer shaped fishes of so many bright rainbow colours were a paradise of enchantment.

The people, especially the Polynesians, are as an attractive a people as one will find anywhere in the world.

That these islands can be claimed by statisticians as amongst the poorest in the world only serves to illustrate how misleading statistics can be. The Polynesians could, in real terms, be classified amongst the fortunate nations of the world, though the Melanesians of the Solomons and New Hebrides live in more primitive, yet passably comfortable conditions.

These people had been well served by a colonial administration which might seem to have been charmingly archaic by British standards, but which was based upon concepts of public service which do not exist in non-colonial countries and which have quickly disappeared in ex-colonial countries. Already the period of colonial rule is acquiring amongst ordinary people an aura of a golden period of peace and integrity.

DEVELOPMENT AID

On my return from my first mission I went to see the Under Secretary responsible for Dependent Territories with three major recommendations. The first was that if we were not to make the tiny islands increasingly dependent upon us we should slow down or reduce the amount of aid available to them. Secondly, we needed to call a meeting to determine the future of these Territories, for with independence the weak administrative links which held them together would be loosened and island loyalties would be likely to lead to a break- up, thus leaving them vulnerable to external predators. Thirdly, that it would be helpful to these colonies or protectorate, that we should provide a couple of economists to help them cope with the modern demanding modalities of aid.

My first suggestion was dismissed "Gordon, do you want to do us out of a job?." I politely refrained from replying. To my second, he said he would think about it – and that is all he ever did. Only the third recommendation was accepted and the islands were set for development.

LOOKING BACK

Nearly 20 years later an annual report produced by the Department of International Development, the renamed Ministry of Overseas Development, expressed regret that there had been such a poor return on the huge amount of aid spent on these countries. In fact most of them were more economically dependent on donors than they ever used to be. I was not surprised.

Meanwhile The Gilbert and Ellice Islands have become two new countries, Kiribati and Tuvalu. The New Hebrides, totally aid-dependent, has become Vanuatu. The Solomons collapsed into inter-island conflict and Australia and New Zealand had to intervene to restore law and order. Fiji has had several coups, primarily to keep the Indian population from controlling the country, and even Tonga has had riots as a new generation questions the old.

Pax Britannica is dead.

Chapter Seven

THE ROAD OF DEATH - BOLIVIA

If you should ever go to Bolivia never take the road to Coroico.

Together with a colleague we were in La Paz, the capital, in the summer of 1962 and had an empty week end before us. The concierge advised us that we should visit Coroico – "Very beautiful, senores – tropical jungle, bananas, many Negros, nice hotel." It sounded a pleasant change from the bleak highlands of the Altiplano so, collecting another United Nations Adviser, we ordered a taxi to take us down for the day.

We were a bit surprised and irritated to find that the taxi driver had brought a friend along, as this meant the three of us had to squeeze into the back seat. We were not entirely convinced by the taxi driver's explanation, " He comes because he knows the way," as it was unlikely to be a destination which had many options. It appeared that it was some 30 miles from La Paz and entailed a drop, down into tropical conditions, of some 6,000 feet.

However, it first entailed going up to 16,000, a height at which oxygen is scarce, and then making one's way down to our tropical paradise.

We started off through the dry, bleak valleys, bright with yellow flowers at that time of the year and full of woolly alpacas and llamas scrambling amongst the scree-strewn valleys. Our driver seemed to be in a great hurry and he perilously raced past huge lorries laden with fruit on top of which many Bolivian peasants travelled precariously on their swaying loads. On more than one occasion he braked suddenly as he was in danger of miscalculating the speed of oncoming cars and at other times he skimmed the edge of the road to get through.

We passed many stone, farm buildings which we were told had been abandoned in the great land reform revolution of 1952 when an uprising of the peasant farmers led to them taking over large holdings in the fertile plains of eastern Bolivia (El Oriente). It had been the first successful land reform in Latin America and most peasants ended up with their own plots. This ensured that when Che Guevara, the Argentine-Cuban leader, came to stir up revolution in 1967 he came to the wrong country, as the peasants were not having another revolution and he was, according to Cuban sources, betrayed by his annoyed Communist colleagues in Bolivia.

Our driver, recklessly in my view, overtook all vehicles until we came to a gravel single-track road and started descending into a deep tree-covered valley. I was sitting by the door overlooking this splendid view when I realized there was only about a foot between it and a vertiginous precipice; the drop was so sheer that as one writer has said, "it would give Chris Bonnington, the climber, sleepless nights". If anything went over the side it would fall for thousands of feet and would be lost forever. There could be no question of rescuing any vehicle or people who went over the edge. I was terrified. There was a pretty good chance with the driver we had that we would go over and never be heard of again.

To make matters worse, visibility was normally only about 50 yards as the road snaked round the mountain outcrops. On the other side of a curve there could be another vehicle coming towards us, and we had seen very few passing places. There was little chance of seeing oncoming vehicles until the last moment.

"Yes, senor," said our co-pilot, "there are many accidents on this road," a remark which seemed totally superfluous as we kept passing memorials to people or vehicles which had disappeared off the road.

But it got worse, for we then entered into clouds and visibility was reduced to about twenty feet. It had one compensation for it was impossible to see how far one would drop if the worst happened.

We were all now wide awake peering through the driver's windscreen hoping to warn him if a vehicle appeared, or to crouch behind the front seat if his reactions were too slow. Eventually it happened, a monstrous truck appeared out of the fog and screeched to a halt a few yards in-front of us. Our driver got out to speak to his opposite number to decide who should give way. Alas our driver was on the downward slope and it was his responsibility to reverse the car to the closest passing bay which was several curves back up the road. We decided to clamber out and inspect the scenery and let him carry out this manoeuvre on his own. His co-pilot did likewise and directed him, like some mad conductor, along the snaking, suicidal road. We now appreciated why he had come.

We were fortunate, for it was late morning and most of the vehicles coming up from the valley had gone through (except those which had gone over the side) and we passed at least ten crosses in the next half hour. Eventually we got below the clouds, and occasionally we were able to see this tortuous road clinging to the massive mountainside in the far distance, and sometimes we could spot traffic coming towards us. Fortunately we only had to repeat the nerve-racking reversing on two more occasions.

Some three hours after we had left, although it seemed an eternity, we arrived shaken but relieved at the bottom of the valley where the promised Eden awaited us. It was indeed a warm tropical valley with a running stream, banana plants and a negro population. One could have been in tropical Africa were it not for the fact that they spoke Spanish. Many must have escaped slavery in migrating to this remote area. It is not commonly known that Simon Bolivar, the great Liberator of South America from the Spaniards, who had been granted a $1million dollars for his efforts by the people of what is now Bolivia and Peru, gave it with remarkable generosity for the purchase of the freedom of 1,000 slaves. Maybe this is where they went.

The hotel, which was our destination, served cold beer and a satisfying lunch which was marred by the thought that we had to make the return journey. This should have started at 1 pm as this was the last hour allowed by the police, but it was 2pm by the time we arrived at the police post. Our driver had omitted to warn us. But the policeman on duty was prepared to allow us through for $1, though he did say it was at our own risk as downward traffic would be on its way.

I was unable to persuade any of my colleagues to sit on the outside seat on the drive back, which was even worse as our driver seemed to go even faster, maybe to get to the top before counter-traffic started down. The clouds were thicker but fortunately we only had to reverse once as the six cars which approached us were all small and passing places were convenient. However, once we were out of the clouds the driver stepped on the accelerator so that his engine kept overheating with the result that we had to stop four times. Finally, at the top of the valley the engine gave up. It was freezing cold and we had to jump up and down to keep warm as the driver fiddled with his clapped-out engine. This took an hour to repair and we arrived back at our hotel cold but much relieved that we had survived the journey. Fortunately the concierge was not on duty; otherwise he might have been unhappy hearing what we thought of his advice.

I learned many years later that the Inter-American Development Bank claimed it as the "most dangerous road in the world". It was stated that over 50 people per year died on it, though how one could count them is impossible to say as once a lorry or a bus went over there was no way of getting to it. Heavens knows how many cars have disappeared off it for there is no way of checking them. Anyone wanting excitement can watch videos on the internet. It makes me feel quite faint seeing the inches which must have separated our taxi wheels from a 6,000 feet drop into the jungle.

So should anyone urge you to visit Coroico, say "no".

BOLIVIA

Bolivia has not had its fair share of luck, neither from nature, nor from man.

Its bleak highland areas have provided a sparse, hard living for Indian communities for many centuries and the majority of the population has been subjected to ruthless exploitation, by the Incas, the Spaniards and the Creoles.

The Incas were hard taskmasters but their irrigation system and agriculture was not as demanding as the silver and tin-mining systems which the Spaniards introduced. The Spaniards forced Indians to work in the mines but so brutal was their treatment of the Indians that only about one in five survived a year. According to one source 2.85 million Indians died working in the mines.

The "black legend" of Spanish rule over the Indians was well merited. William Miller, one of the key figures in the independence battles wrote:

"Volumes might be written upon the endless varieties of oppression, both secular and ecclesiastical, which reduced this hapless race to a condition of wretchedness, in comparison with which that of the negro slave is a state of comfort."

Indians were obliged to work in the mines or on farms for Spaniards for nominal sums of money which were seldom paid, and were linked to loans for food, which made them slaves for life. Governors and priests were allowed to have free servants and there were tens of thousands who had to perform this role. They were also ruthlessly exploited by Governors who had a monopoly of trade goods which they sold at huge mark-ups, often goods Indians did not want. One story is told of a Governor who had hundreds of unwanted spectacles which he could not sell, so he made wearing of spectacles compulsory in church and Indians were forced to buy them.

"One curate of moderate living in the province of Quito advised that he received during the year, as presents which he exacted at certain festivals, 200 sheep, 6,000 head of poultry, 4,000 guinea pigs and 50,000 eggs."

The same authority states of the clergy "The scandalous example afforded by their licentiousness was still more pernicious than their avarice" and "When Indians were unable to repeat from memory prayers they did not understand, they were often publicly whipped at the church porch."

A priest who had buried an Indian demanded of his wife that she should pay fees for the burial and, when she could not, insisted that she give him her eight- year- old son as a slave.

Bolivia's incredibly rich silver mines served to benefit the Spaniards and enslave the Indians.

Independence from Spain in 1825 and the establishment of a state named after its principal emancipator, Bolivar, resulted in theory in the abolition of forced labour and the many restrictions on the Indian population.

GENERAL WILLIAM MILLER

Even if you ask educated people in Bolivia who William Miller was, you are almost certain to get a blank look. He was a young English soldier from Kent. In his day he was one of the great heroes of the independence movement. He was a General in the patriot army at the age of 29 and he led the cavalry in the final and crucial charge which defeated the Spaniards at the last battle, at Ayacucho, in the war for independence, in 1825.

He was the only non- South American amongst the four generals who participated in the battle.

Seven years earlier Miller had joined the Argentine army in Chile at the age of 20, having previously served in the British army. His ability, courage, daring and leadership qualities made him popular, and indeed lucky, as he was wounded seven times. He accompanied General San Martin from Chile to Peru where they sought to defeat the centre of Spanish power on the continent.

His guerrilla tactics became legendary, and his ability to coax the best out of the ragged bands of soldiers made his units popular and successful.

The ultimate accolade in leadership for a "gringo" must surely be leading the wildest and best horsemen in the world, the gauchos of South America. As he says in his autobiography "they were the most ragged, wildest bunch he had ever commanded, but they were the best". There was a cavalry battle before that of Ayacucho in which he and his gauchos defeated the Spaniards without a shot being fired. It was a battle of lancers in which speed, skill and courage won the day.

Once victory was won, the real problems of government began and Miller was appointed the Governor of Potosi in 1826. Thanks to tin mines the district was the key to the new country's economy.

He was a man with great administrative skills, with energy and principles. The previous quotations were all taken from his book and they highlight his concern for some of the most oppressed people in the world. The wicked restrictions and enforcements on Indians were all declared illegal and he did everything possible to ensure that abuses did not continue, even to the extent of having soldiers, who mistreated Indians, flogged. But laws are not enough and mistreatment of Indians after independence continued despite the efforts of the more principled leaders of the independence movement.

He was also active in carrying out reforms, reducing huge Spanish salaries, instituting courts, building roads and doubling tin production.

Alas this paragon only administered this huge district for a year, as his wounds were causing him problems and he had to return to England for treatment.

Had Bolivia been able to produce more Governors of his integrity and competence it would have had a very different history. Alas, independence brought to Bolivia, and indeed all the Latin countries, decades of anarchy as the interests of individuals, families and groups overrode the national interest. The public sector was there to be plundered. The idea of public service has been alien to the Spanish cultural inheritance. Bolivia, after over a century of independence had had more Governments than years of freedom from Spain.

Conflicts with neighbouring countries added to their problems and pieces of the country disappeared into the maws of Chile, Brazil and Paraguay. While independence had given the majority Indian population legal rights, these were seldom enforced and many of the old abuses continued. The main beneficiaries of the independence movement were the new Creole class, those of mixed European and Indian blood.

It was only in 1952, as mentioned above, that Indians were able to seize a more equitable share of the nations scarce resources The feudal land- holding system which they had inherited from Spain was destroyed and the land shared out amongst the peasants. This was the first major land reform in South America.

This ushered in a period of relative democracy and economic development and they even had the same President for seven years in the late 1960s. Admittedly it was not all that a democratic regime, the President's name Banzer, suggesting German "efficiency" genes, but the economy flourished and the peasants were quiet, though troubles continued in the mines where trade unions clashed with the state owners.

TRAVEL IN BOLIVIA

Bolivia has the geographical advantage of being on the boundary of the great historical attraction in Peru of Cuzco, an Inca and colonial gem of a town, and the great Inca fortress of Machu Pichu. A short train ride southwards gets one to the largest lake in South America, Lake Titicaca, with its reed boats and reed islands and onto the bleak plains of the Altiplano. Their vastness also fascinates and one wonders how anyone can survive on these burning hot and freezing cold flatlands. The answer has been the potato. It has its origin in the Andes and there it is a poor creature, small and twisted. It is a miracle of science that turned it into the product which transformed food production in Europe. In the Andes it is mashed up and left overnight in the open which freezes it into a product which can be stored for future consumption. It is worth trying some, if only to be thankful to western scientists who have made it edible.

The pre-Colombian ruins at Tiahuanaco near Lake Titicaca are a reminder that there was a culture before the Incas destroyed it.

La Paz, the capital has a reasonably attractive nineteenth-century boulevard and some buildings of baroque charm, but most of the city is a modern concrete jumble of architectural styles of little merit. However, the many colourful markets full of Indians selling charms, pots, ponchos, plastic goods, and llama embryos are a delightful mix of medieval and modern. There are still many Indian women in their huge colourful skirts wearing bowler hats and sometimes white top hats, to remind one that the world is different. Most curious is their choice of musical instruments considering the oxygen shortage. They are essentially woodwind, with which they blow haunting melodies, alas now not unique as they are heard on most of our High Streets.

The least- known urban gem of Bolivia is the one-time capital Sucre. It is a splendidly preserved colonial jewel of a town. The buildings are colonial, with beautiful red tiled roofs, no concrete buildings have been allowed, and, there are no buildings of any type over two storeys in height. It has beautiful plazas and churches, and is well preserved. It is probably one of the finest colonial towns in South America, certainly the best I have seen.

Their churches are full of decorated saints and the Catholic church has absorbed many Indian beliefs. Though if the admission by an Indian woman whom I met on a bus is anything to go by, the Catholic Church is not all that popular. I had asked the woman what religion she practised and she said that " We are all Catholic." And then rather daringly for an Indian she said to me, "And what is your religion Sir ?" I replied in a vague agnostic sort of way that there could be a god somewhere, and I think I must have waved at the sun but I was not a Catholic "Ah sir," she said "That is what we think. The priests here are all rogues. They charge $4, $6, $8 for a marriage, $2 for a baptism, $20 for a funeral. Depends on what you pay. Yes I believe in a God alright, that of the sun and the moon, and that all the evils in the world of beetles, fleas were brought on by our own sins". She echoed the complaints of Indians about the clergy which William Miller records in his account of Bolivia 125 years earlier.

It is not surprising that evangelical churches have made huge inroads into traditional societies as they offer a strict code of family behaviour, condemning alcoholism and adultery and providing strong social and moral support. They have been hugely successful in urban areas where there has been great geographical mobility.

Before joining the British Government I had been able to visit Bolivia twice, once on an official United Nation advisory visit, and later on a visit with Jean to that "Mecca" of South America, Machu Picchu and Cuzco, which led us over Lake Titicaca in a paddle boat built in Manchester in 1905, to the medieval markets of La Paz. It was this background which shaped my subsequent actions in dealing with Latin America.

AIDING BOLIVIA

With the rather grand title of Senior Economic Adviser for Latin America in the British Ministry of Overseas Development, I had considerable flexibility and influence in decision- making as none of the administrators responsible for the programme knew anything about Latin America. When I recommended that we should direct most of our efforts to Bolivia, the poorest of the countries, this was accepted without question.

In order to identify which sectors in Bolivia, and which organisations, merited British aid (all of which came in the form of a grant to purchase British goods) I had to work up a programme which promoted the development of the country and which would ensure the aid was properly spent. No easy task in a disorganised country such as Bolivia.

The amount of funds we had to allocate was fairly flexible but in today's currency would have been between £15m and £20m .This was a generous contribution towards a country in which Britain had no real political or commercial interest. It was a purely humanitarian gesture though some might argue that it was tied to the acquisition of British goods. There were two answers to this. The first was that the aid was a grant so it was no burden to the recipient, and if it had not been tied to British goods the recipients could have used the aid to acquire US or other foreign goods, which would hardly be fair.

To implement this programme I had to visit Bolivia in the company of other experts in order to determine how best we could help. I was usually accompanied on these missions by agricultural or engineering advisers.

There were two main problems in developing an aid programme in Bolivia. The first was getting Bolivian civil servants to turn up on time, or even to see us at all. There was nothing personal about this, they just had no concept of punctuality, or administrative discipline. On more than one occasion I walked off with my team after having been kept waiting for more than half an hour. The Bolivians were all quite charming and pleasant, they just had no idea that it might be inconvenient for someone if they did not turn up.

When one added to this the fact that many of the offices were on top floors with lifts that did not work in a capital city almost 10,000 feet above sea level, one's physique, as well as one's patience, was sorely tested.

More important however, was the huge competition from other countries and international agencies offering aid. Every Ministry we visited had aid projects being implemented or about to be signed which stretched their generally inefficient administration to the limit. The World Bank and USAID had huge projects in agriculture.

The World Bank had the road sector all tied up, the Inter- American Development Bank was dealing with power projects, the EC helping with water development, other donors were investing in telecommunications. Every Government Department had as many, if not more, aid offers than they could cope with.

We were able to offer manpower assistance for agricultural projects, and in fact established a small research station in the grasslands of the east, and later we provided a geological team to carry out a survey of the little-known eastern region.

This competition for sound aid projects everywhere in the world had become well established by the mid and late 1970s and the term " lack of absorptive capacity" was one we professionals were encountering everywhere. It was not the response our liberal political masters wished to hear for they had convinced themselves that the problems of developing countries could be solved by providing increasing quantities of aid. Since the amount of aid contributed by most rich countries was only a tiny proportion of their GNP, aid lobbies, and those who became politically influential, devoted their efforts to increasing the percentage of aid to the figure of 0.7% of GNP which had been agreed as a target years before by the United Nations. This target was never met, and indeed had it been there would have been a massive waste of aid funds.

These targets for annual disbursement were, fortunately for us in the British Aid Programme, never rigidly enforced so we could adjust to the circumstances of each country. In the World Bank country targets were determined by the President and under McNamara a new dynamic President, they were carefully monitored by computer so that desk officers were obliged to do everything possible to meet them. This had disastrous consequences as any ambitious Desk Officer had to meet these targets regardless of the impact on the recipient country. As a result World Bank Projects were all too often over- designed, over-optimistic, much too large, and many failed.

While there were no pressures on me to allocate funds to projects, I had to think imaginatively about what Britain might usefully do to help Bolivia. The lack of obvious needy sectors or ministries in Bolivia obliged me to take a look at the one sector every donor had ignored as it was thought to be too political and too incompetent, yet it was Bolivia's most important economic activity: mining.

Mining came under a State Corporation and all reports condemned it as an inefficient and far too politically driven an organisation to assist. However I thought it merited an evaluation so I organised a small team composed of a very experienced mining engineer, a geologist and myself, to check out the State Mining Corporation.

We were very impressed by a young team of mining engineers whom we met and even more impressed when we visited their tin mines to find they were actually managing their machinery very well, considering that it was all at least 50 years old. Our mining engineer got very excited to see this museum actually working. He pointed out that simple equipment such as compressors, drills, and cables were years past their safe-to-use date and were all very dangerous, yet they were being efficiently used. He thought a re-equipment programme was essential, and Britain could provide it.

Meanwhile, I was aware of the appalling working conditions and our need to be seen to do something for workers and asked to see their housing facilities. To this day I remember being ashamed and embarrassed when shown round, a comfortably off gringo voyeur, witnessing living quarters in which in one case six men were sharing a room, two per bed. In another there were eight in a room. They were appalling conditions. The men's eyes seem to light up at the thought that someone was going to do something about their conditions.

This gave me an idea. I proposed that the grant we would make available to the Bolivian Government for mine re-equipment should be passed on to the State Mining Corporation in the form of a loan at 5% on condition that the interest should be spent on improved housing and mining welfare conditions. The managers of the State Mining Corporation accepted the idea enthusiastically.

We therefore immediately wrote out terms of reference for a feasibility study which would identify up to £15m of British equipment to be used for the refurbishment of the tin mines. It was agreed there and then but it required Bolivian Ministerial approval, so to give them an incentive I told that if they sent us a formal request within two weeks, we would have a team back in Bolivia within three months to identify the equipment required.

Miraculously their formal request appeared in two weeks and we sent out a team within the prescribed period. They returned with a project worth £12m which I quickly wrote up and submitted to our Capital Projects Committee who approved it.

Then disaster struck. The Head of Catholic Relief in Latin America heard that Britain was approving a project to aid "the fascist regime in Bolivia". Worse than that, it was a project to help the State Mining Corporation which had suppressed a strike and sent some of the Chilean strikers back to Chile, which under the Pinochet regime would not have received them hospitably.

Great pressure was put on our left-leaning Minister by the Catholic Relief Agency to cancel this "outrageous support for a fascist regime." I had to appear before the Minister as she explained that she had been approached by a delegation of exiled Bolivian workers, "very nice little people, and" "she assured me who objected to our aiding this "fascist regime." I explained to her that our project was designed to help the workers. The mines were the most dangerous our mining adviser had ever seen and re-equipment should save many lives and prevent even more injuries and said that I had secured agreement that £600,000 a year would go into improved workers conditions.

Alas, nothing would shake her and she refused to support the project. She proposed that I go back to Bolivia and identify a politically less " sensitive" project.

I did go back but the health sector which I identified was a bureaucracy too far. The equipment required needed to be suited to Bolivian conditions, and the scattered nature of their requirements and the administrative confusion were too difficult to overcome.

I often wonder how many lives could have been saved by the mining project and how many workers lives made more comfortable had it gone ahead ?. I also wonder whether the blinkered objectors were ever aware of the harm they did to many poor workers in Bolivia.

Chapter Eight

A VERY UNUSUAL CONFERENCE

"Gordon" said the Under Secretary for Africa, "can you accompany me to the UN Economic Commission for Africa's Annual Conference next month?"

My heart sank. I had attended several of these United Nations regional conferences in Latin America and Africa and I knew that they were no more than forums for Ministers from the region to make lengthy, boring speeches about the splendid way in which they were managing their economies, which their national press would publicise. None of them would have bothered to read the worthy documents about the state of Latin America or Africa which I and many UN staff had laboured over, and if any ex-colonial power was unwise enough to participate there would be an outpouring of indignation about the wrongs of imperialism and how their present problems were the result of this heritage. Worse still this conference was to be in Lagos, a steamy ugly, chaotic, stewpot, of a town.

I had also attended United Nations Conferences in Europe (where the gossip defined a "Developing Country" as one which paid its attendees $100 a day. The going rate was around $30 – which was quite generous) and found that the British Team Leader seldom participated in debate.

There had been an occasion, however, when I was the Leader of the British delegation, and only British participant, when the British delegation made a real impact on the conference. This was a World Bank meeting in Dar es Salaam to discuss Tanzania's performance, and I was let out on my own largely because no one wanted to go to Dar es Salaam, which is incidentally an attractive port town, and also because it was not that important a meeting.

On that occasion I really enjoyed myself by making some very helpful suggestions about the better running of the rundown, sclerotic Tanzanian economy. One of my memorable suggestions was that they should remove or reduce the huge taxes on farm products and pay farmers much higher prices, and instead of providing free, badly managed state run education, let the farmers pay for their children's education. Since farmers knew very well how important education was they would be keen to send their children to school and ensure that they got value for money. This would mean a much more efficient system of agriculture and of education. This bit of pre -Thatcher free market advice was received with an icy silence rather than abuse. Since, twenty years later, Tanzania became a far more efficient market led economy, it may well have been possible that young Tanzanian attendees at the Conference may have heeded my wise counsel.

Of more immediate impact at this conference were the comments of an attractive young English interpreter who accosted me at cocktails that evening to say that she was normally embarrassed and ashamed to have to translate dreary statements by British Delegates but on this occasion my interventions had cheered her up no end and made her "proud to be British." It's curious how this tiny, timely and unusual compliment has survived in my memory after many decades of dreary meetings.

But what was I to say to my Under Secretary? I would have to write most of his briefs, and he was most unlikely to stick his head over the parapet by actually speaking at an African conference – but he was an excellent Under Secretary, had fought as a Major at the battle of Monte Cassino, and unlike several of his colleagues actually asked for economic advice from time to time.

"Of course, Dick," I said, "I would be delighted to accompany you – even to Lagos." This was diplomacy, tact and politeness, not lies or hypocrisy. After all he was my boss.

I had a feeling that not all was going to go well when I met John, our Foreign Office "minder" at the airport. He was there to ensure that we, in the subordinate Department of Overseas Development, did not provoke a conflict between the African nations and Britain, and to ensure that we won friends and influenced people. He was a tall, thin tight-lipped unsmiling character who could easily, if wearing a monocle, have been a Nazi Commandant in a TV comedy.

This suspicion was confirmed when we arrived at Lagos Airport where we were met by a friendly Nigerian official who to our surprise had allocated us two shiny Mercedes Benz. This was splendidly generous gesture which only poor countries seem to be able to make. This pleased John, no end, and he informed me that the second car " is my car – but we can share it".

My education in diplomatic protocol was enhanced when he informed me that the "senior seat" in the car was that behind the driver, and he made sure that I did not usurp his authority by clambering in first.

Our car set off at speed from the airport. Alas, it did not have air conditioning and the car windows were open. It was also unfortunate that "John's" driver had not been instructed in diplomatic hygiene, let alone elementary physics, for he suddenly decided to clear his throat, which he did with great vigour, and spat out of the window. The missile did not get very far as we were travelling fast and within a second it had re-entered by the rear window of the car and collided with our senior diplomat's right eye. "My god," he screamed "I've been hit." Considering the unpleasantness of the experience I must say his reaction was surprisingly restrained.

Whenever I feel depressed, or at a dull dinner party, thinking of or recounting this incident restores my good humour and entertains others.

The conference itself turned out as I had forecast, a parade of Ministers telling us what a splendid job they were doing, and if it had not been for trade restrictions by metropolitan powers, unfair debts and insufficient aid, they could have done far better.

John meanwhile pursued his autocratic behaviour. At the conference he turned on me, "Your briefcase is open;" he informed me accusingly. "So what?" I replied. He went on "It contains confidential papers and regulations say that they must be kept secure. They are not." Since I had written most of this "confidential" material, full of spirited ripostes to possible African accusations of unfair agricultural restrictions in Europe (European agricultural producers are temperate and Africa's tropical so there is no effect) , or on indebtedness (had the loans been used for their original purpose they could have been repaid) , I thought his reprimand rather tiresome, but in the interest of peace I snapped my briefcase shut.

Things changed dramatically for the better for John when Dick told us that he was going to host a lunch for all Heads of Commonwealth Delegations. John was to organise it. John was thrilled. It was all about "placement" he told me. Did I realize how important it was to sit the right people at dinner in the right place ? A slip-up could lead to a diplomatic dust up; a break in relations if one's country was insulted by placing their representative beside the wrong person . Many diplomatic careers had, so he told me, had been ruined by incompetent " placement" skills.

He kept away from me for some days to my great relief and when the great luncheon day came he said, " Gordon, would you go to the Hotel entrance and direct the guests to the lunch." I accepted this doorkeeper role slightly resentfully but with a smile, surprised that he was including me in the lunch. The problem I faced at the door was that there were stacks of people coming in and I had no way of knowing who was the High Commissioner from the country invited. I followed the "precautionary principle"; if he looked affluent and diplomatic I said, "The Commonwealth lunch is on the left." There seemed to be quite a lot of people who looked like High Commissioners and who were very interested to hear of the lunch.

When I left my post, five minutes before the start of the lunch, there was a heaving mass of people in the dining room with a white-faced John trying to persuade many rather indignant, crestfallen characters that this free lunch was not for them. It was a happy moment for me.

Better still, was that when I found my allocated seat in a distant corner of the table, most of the dining room had been cleared of disappointed, sometimes angry free-loaders and only John was left standing. " Ho John" said one of the seated High Commissioners, " where are you sitting ?". There was no place left for John.

Back at the Conference John kept saying to me, "Why don't you participate in the conference and say something ?" This struck a rather more responsive chord. I would love to have said something, indeed I would love to have said a lot. Give me twenty minutes on the podium and I would have set out a programme to save Africa. But it was Dick whose job it was to speak – not mine. And there was no way that he, or anyone, was going to lecture African Ministers in public on how to manage their economies.

But his nagging did spark off the next incident. After a few days of lethargic, bored attendance I was able to persuade Dick that as he and John were very competent they could surely do without me and since I had urgent issues in London needing attention, I could leave the conference early.

It was a very hot humid Tuesday afternoon at the conference as there was no air conditioning. Only about half of the attendees were there and most were sound asleep as the speaker, who seemed half asleep, droned on and the Chairman himself dozed fitfully. My flight was at night so I thought it would be a good idea to go back to my hotel for a snooze.

Even John was sound asleep, snoring gently, as I quietly stepped over his legs and slipped out. "Our", sorry, "his" car was there so I asked the driver to take me back to the hotel where I fell into a beautiful slumber.

I was awoken by a thundering on the door; must be a fire I thought. The banging went on. I eventually got up and drowsily opened the door. There was John incandescent with fury. "You took my car" he sceamed. "You left the Conference without telling me. I have had to walk back."

I realized with inward joy that "his" driver had not gone back to fetch him. I was in no mood to put up with him and I used a very rude phrase which included "off" and quietly closed the door. However, I did not succeed for he charged it and burst into my room, his face red with fury, his body jerking violently and he seemed to be about to hit me in blind fury ."You are a disgrace," he was able to scream. "You are a disgrace to the country. You have been useless, incompetent". He roared on. I was in underpants and so toned down my riposte to " oh do go away". Eventually fuming he retreated shouting that he was going to report my appalling behaviour to the Foreign Secretary.

I never saw him again but many years later he hit the headlines of the Sunday papers as Britain's beleaguered Ambassador in one of the most distant and unpleasant countries in the world. Clearly the Foreign Office had hoped that they had seen the end of him when they sent him there.

Chapter Nine

MISSION TO THE MALDIVES

"The RAF are abandoning their air base at Gann", said the Senior Administrative Officer responsible for the Pacific and Indian Ocean Territories, " could you lead a mission to agree on how to spend the £3m we have allocated the islanders as compensation?"

I thought I had better not enquire where on earth Gann was or point out that to find alternative occupations for islanders accustomed to a living funded by the Armed Forces would be no easy task, as he might question my competence. So without hesitation I assured him that such an assignment could be in no better hands.

"What about getting there? Can I get to Gann?" I asked cautiously hoping that this would be a clue to where it was. "No chance," was the reply, " the base has closed down and anyhow this has to be negotiated with the Government. " I was learning – there was a Government somewhere – but where? "You will need to fly to Sri Lanka – and there is an occasional flight to Male where you will have to negotiate a deal with the Government of the Maldives."

Well I had heard of the Maldives as being somewhere in the Indian Ocean, so it sounded quite interesting and £3m in those days was quite a reasonable sum (about a tenth of what it would be worth now).

We discussed putting together a team – we needed a civil engineer, and since there seemed to be a lot of water in the region a fisheries adviser seemed sensible. I would also take the desk officer as he would have to implement the programme for without his support no programme was ever likely to move forward.

Unfortunately the Fisheries Adviser was not going to be available so we had to make do without him.

The Foreign Office, our senior partners, then decided to send their desk 0fficer as well. This scarcely seemed essential but since none of their staff had ever been to the Maldives it was not an unreasonable suggestion.

Being a mission Leader is not always an easy task but this was a small team, although having a Foreign Office "minder" along was slightly disconcerting as he might not agree with our findings or our actions. The civil engineer was a lively, able, cockney with few diplomatic pretensions and our own desk officer was a quiet, amiable, junior administrator unlikely to rock the boat.

My first "management" problem was how to deal with the suggestion made by John, the civil engineer, that I should ask that we should all be allowed to travel first class. By rank, I was the only one entitled to do so but he informed me that there was a regulation that allowed for upgrading "if it was essential for an exchange of ideas on a mission". This was tricky – as it would obviously be in my interest to have a happy band of followers with me, but how on earth could I credibly persuade the administration that this was a reasonable request? No way. I thought for a while of downgrading my own ticket and become "one of the boys" but I had done this once with a very large team and got no thanks for it – and in fact they were the most unruly team I had ever led. Anyhow I had only just returned from Sri Lanka and was darned if I was going all that way again economy class. I told them the request had been turned down.

So off we went to Sri Lanka. We spent a day in Colombo the capital, to be briefed about the Maldives by the British High Commissioner (or Ambassador). I had by this time checked in the reference library about the Maldives but there was very little about them – 2,000 islands, 19 atolls and a population of 123,000 was all I was able to find out, and it was a republic. The High Commission was no more informative and the visit a complete waste of time.

Meanwhile George, our "minder", seemed to be becoming just a little neurotic. He was a pleasant, balding middle-aged chap and his assignment to this part of the world in the Foreign Office could not be deemed a career move. He was nothing like my previous Foreign Office "minder" on the assignment to Nigeria.

But back to George. He was quite amiable but started to show an obsession with "security". This meant that we had to ensure that any papers we'd unwisely brought with us marked "Confidential" were kept within locked briefcases and never left our person. It was unfortunate that I had brought our "briefing" with me – all it was was a page telling us to identify projects, which would compensate for the loss of income from the RAF withdrawal. Nothing useful about the social, political or economic structure of the Republic of the Maldives. But this meant that if I left my brief case open, or went to the loo without it, George told me off.

Our next flight was in a frayed, small, half empty, Avro 748, which, after a two-hour flight bounced us onto a very primitive airstrip on a tiny island in the Maldives. There was no passenger terminal building on this island site, no passport control, let alone immigration control. Quite unique even for those times. It was late in the evening when we arrived but the bright white sand and the heat welcomed us to our tropical destination. Our bags were carried to a tiny quay where a speedboat awaited us and sped us to the only hotel in the Maldives, situated on another island about 20 minutes away.

The hotel, based on the charmingly named island of Wilingini, was the only resort for visitors at that time. It was a generous timber structure set amongst palm trees on the beach which even at night sparkled white.

Relaxing over a drink in the bar we were approached by a well-dressed bulky, self- assured Indian gentleman who asked, "Are you the British Delegation?" When he was assured that we were none other, he announced "I have just come from seeing the President and he tells me that you are going to build a new port for Male" (this was the capital).

This was news to us and not very welcome as we were supposed to be helping the people of Gann – who were 600 miles south of Male.

When I pointed this out to him there was a surprised and even pained look on his face "That lot," he said, – "they have had lots of money as a British base, no chance of the President agreeing to more. – a subversive lot – no chance of them getting anything, the rest hate them." He claimed that the once privileged inhabitants of Gann had sought secession from the Republic, but now it was payback time and they would get nothing.

I could not help reflecting that had we had better briefing from the Foreign Office we probably would not have been here at all, but it was too late to turn back.

The Indian businessman, for that's what he turned out to be, enlightened us on quite a number of useful background facts. There was a Ministry of Political Crimes which ensured that the Maldives were well run, streets kept clean and that there was no dissent from the President's wishes. Those careless enough to indicate any were immediately despatched to one of the many uninhabited islands of the "Republic" and the President was "of course" president for life. The country was moderately prosperous thanks to trading and maritime activities across the Indian Ocean and, of course, due to the rich fishing grounds in the vicinity. Tourism held out hopes for future prosperity and the airstrip we had so precariously negotiated was being upgraded to take international flights. He left us in a reflective mood – particularly wondering what the Foreign Office were for.

We had a meeting scheduled with the Foreign Minister at noon the following day so there was nothing more we could do. George looked rather glum and we sought to cheer him up about what looked like a magnificent cock- up, which could have been avoided had the Foreign Office been up to date on domestic politics, but his glumness turned out to be due to another cause. He had been caught with his briefcase open at the British High Commission by their security guard in Colombo and this would be duly recorded on his file. When we laughed he went off his rocker with fury at our lack of sympathy. His career was ruined he moaned. We quickly apologised for our lack of understanding and I assured him I would send in a splendid report to his boss on our return about his cooperation and competence.

I awoke next morning to a glorious sight. Outside my bedroom veranda was a glistening white beach shaded by palm trees and fringing a turquoise, clear sea. Grabbing my goggles I meandered through thousands of tiny land crabs and within seconds I was in a cool, refreshing translucent blue sea. Fishes of rainbow colours – bright red, bright yellow, black, some of the weirdest shapes with long tails, and fancy fins drifted around quite unconcernedly. One of them attached itself to me as if I were a mother fish – they were unbelievably tame.

The coral was of every conceivable shape – some like cobwebs, others like cabbages, others weirdly like human brains – and the colours ranged from purple to green. Huge open scallop shells closed suddenly as I swam over them.

All of a sudden I was at the edge of the reef and its near vertical wall, covered all the way down with gently swaying exotic plants, was brushed by myriads of coloured fish many of them yards long. They had no fear of this intrusive flapping object swimming amongst them.

It was certainly the most exciting underwater sea scene I had ever encountered – and this included visits to many Pacific and Caribbean islands.

Clearly the Maldives had a tourist potential, provided its potentially disruptive social and economic effects were handled carefully.

Just before noon a motor launch turned up and in 20 minutes we were on island number three, the capital Male. It turned out to be a pleasantly developed Arab trading port – narrow, sandy streets, shady lanes one or two- storey houses, virtually no cars but lots of bicycles. We noted a bus which seemed very out of place and it turned to be one of two that had been commandeered from Gann by the Government for a free school run. Their main problem was that the children lived so near to their schools and so enjoyed the trip that they ran back to the assembly point before the bus returned, creating an almost endless bus facility.

On arrival at the quay we were told that the Foreign Ministry was 200 yards away so I thought we would walk. But George was not having this; he put his Foreign Office foot down and said it would be most unbecoming of Her Majesty's Representatives to turn up on foot. He insisted we take the lone taxi. I thought I had better check the price of this proposal and was staggered to be told by the driver that it would be £30 - many times that in today's currency. Conscious of the dignity of this first British Mission to the Maldives I decided not to quibble, and hope that the accountants back home would pay this outrageous piece of blackmail, so we all clambered in to be debouched a few seconds later at the Maldivian Foreign Office.

A small, dapper, blue-suited Foreign Minister, in a large, carpeted, fan- cooled office, received us courteously. After an exchange of pleasantries I explained our reasons for visiting this "exquisite Indian ocean pearl" (my colleagues said I had missed a diplomatic vocation). The Foreign Minister then explained that they needed a new international port at Male – as the businessman had predicted – and they proposed to use our funds for this purpose.

I was about to respond as tactfully as possible to explain that this was not possible, when John, ignoring protocol, let alone tact, jumped in. He told the Minister that not only was this not possible and that they did not need such a large facility and spent about five minutes explaining why this was so. I was able to hide my irritation at his premature intervention, though this was mollified by knowing that I agreed with him and that he would take the flack.

The Minister listened somewhat stunned and then excused himself. He reappeared about half an hour later, presumably having consulted his boss, clutching a hand written note, which he proceeded to read out.

The substance was that since we refused to fund a new harbour there was no point in us continuing our discussions and they were therefore at end. There was no point in us staying here.

Out of the corner of my eye I saw George go white at the thought of being involved in an international imbroglio which might be interpreted as a Foreign Office own goal. .On the other hand it occurred to me that in 1978 a beleaguered Labour Government might well welcome the diversion of an international standoff with a petty dictator. However, I thought of George returning in shame and decided to play the diplomat. I explained to the Minister that he might have misunderstood John's intervention – the British Government would not wish to dispute the Presidents judgement but what we wanted to ensure was that they got the right sort of port which entailed examining a series of options from minor improvements to the major solution which they were searching for. To this end we were prepared to fund a British Ports consultancy to evaluate their needs and make recommendations – omitting to mention that we would tell the Consultants that their recommendations should result in minimal improvements.

This took the heat out of the issue and the Foreign Minister trotted off to check with his boss to see if this was acceptable.

The next day or so was spent discussing terms of reference for the study and lying horizontally on the Indian Ocean marvelling at the coloured variety and shapes of tropical sea life and imagining that in the not- too- far future these tropical jewels would became a tourist magnet. Later I took a walk along the beach. After about an hour I was stunned to find that there was another hotel on the island only to discover that I had done a circular tour of the island and had "discovered" my own hotel.

I then decided that I had had enough of George's obsessions with my confidential documents and I would get rid of them. So I tore them up in little bits and flushed them down the loo hoping they would not emerge legibly in the lagoon. They did not. They refused to be washed down the pan. There they floated defiantly in front of me. There was nothing for it but to retrieve them and I squashed them into a tight ball and later when George was not looking threw them out of our motorboat into the big wide blue sea.

At midnight there was a full moon and in its bright white sandy reflections I was able to write up my diary on the quiet empty beach.

Next day we heard that our proposals for the port study were acceptable. Not exactly what we had been sent out to achieve but better than nothing.

Next day we were off. Eventually Her Majesty's Government wrote an unusually strong letter to H.E.The President of the Maldives agreeing to the ports study but informing him that unless these funds were used to a considerable extent to assist the people of Gann they would not be made available.

I never heard what happened to George but I did not come across him again. It is possible that his career was blighted, though I did send the Foreign Office a memo thanking them for his valued participation. As for aid to the people of Gann – I moved to other theatres of endeavour and never heard whether it reached them. I expect not.

Chapter Ten

RISE AND FALL

I was once again trying to adapt myself to the oxygen- deficient atmosphere in La Paz, Bolivia. I was on yet another mission to investigate the possibility of using the loan which the Minister had so unwisely (in my opinion) rejected in favour of the provision of assistance of health equipment to the many needy hospitals. I received a call from H.M. Ambassador. I wondered why he wished to see me – he had put no obstacles in my way of offering the Bolivians the mining loan and I had been splendidly diplomatic when, on an earlier visit he had informed me that Bolivia's geographical position made it the most important of all South American countries. This remarkable observation rather surprised me. If so, it had certainly been upgraded since Queen Victoria's days. When she was told that her Ambassador had been made to ride on a donkey backwards, she ordered Bolivia to "be struck off the map". I unkindly wondered whether this new policy made him the most important Ambassador on the continent. Naturally I did not utter such a cynical thought but marvelled at his wisdom.

However, that was not why he had called me into his splendid office. I have often wondered how British Ambassadors in distant countries spend their time. We had had some excellent chats in the past about the world but on this occasion he merely handed me a confidential Telex (yes, it was that long ago) from my London office which said: "This is to confirm that you have been selected for the post of Director of the Geographical Division of the Economic Planning Staff". Oh yes, it politely added "Congratulations".

This was the Division in which I had been working for the last seven years and I was now to be responsible for thirty economists, the second largest congregation of economists in Whitehall, who were provided to administrators of the seventy or so countries which we aided. In theory it was a considerable responsibility and naturally the pay rise was very welcome.

I was a bit surprised that I had been selected as in the past senior posts had been filled by eminent outsiders. Presumably it had at last sunk in that academics seldom adapted well to the practical world of decision- making in the public service, and they had gone for a more practical option – experience rather than eminence.

I could not help reflecting on the fragile nature of the views of one's seniors. Two years earlier I had been persuaded by a journalist friend to help him write a book to dispute the fears, which were being fanned in the USA, that the world was heading for starvation, a view I had vigorously challenged when having a drink with him. We entitled it "Famine in Retreat". He did the writing, I did the thinking. When I submitted this popular account to the Chief Economist for his approval I was taken aback when he called me in and told me "This is not going to advance your professional career." It had never occurred to me think of it as a career enhancing effort. It is true it had a jocular, journalese style which could irritate intellectuals, but it had a serious educational role which I thought merited publication. Fortunately it was approved, was very well reviewed and we even received letters of congratulation from U Thant, the Secretary General of the United Nations, and Robert McNamara, President of the World Bank.

Maybe it was because our then Chief Economist had moved on that I had been promoted. Maybe the penny had at last sunk in that "transplants" did not thrive. Maybe there was no one better around. I was quite touched when I returned to Britain (alas the attempt to help hospitals in Bolivia foundered in the swamps of Bolivian bureaucracy) when several members of my new staff expressed pleasure "that one of us had been promoted", and hoped this enthusiasm was not influenced by the vacancies this created down the line, or the hope that I would be able to enhance their careers.

The economists coming under my responsibility were some of the brightest and best in Whitehall because overseas development was second only to the Treasury as the most attractive Government department in the Government Economic Service. However, while I had professional responsibility for them, they were, to use current jargon, "embedded" in the country departments which they advised, or were seconded to embassies abroad. This was a sensible management decision but it meant I had a limited influence over their work, and especially so as all their economic appraisals of projects, which ran to several hundreds of millions of pounds per year, went for approval to a Projects Committee over which my seniors, not I, presided. Our economists were extremely well trained in the techniques of cost/benefit analysis; perhaps too well, as too much time was spent on creating financial models based upon very dubious data, while most of the projects requiring analysis, such as schools, airports, surveys, had no financial outputs and required a more practical approach to their appraisal.

Most of my efforts in my new role were of a didactic nature, producing practical guidelines for my staff on how to appraise proposals which did not allow for conventional cost/ benefit techniques, (which eventually led to a book written with a very able and literate colleague: "Planning Development Projects"), producing country policy papers, seeking to ensure the aid allocation to countries was appropriate and properly forecast, and dealing with international institutions.

THE AID FRAMEWORK

Once a year I, the Director, had to produce an "ideal" allocation of Britain's country aid programmes, (known as the Aid Framework) recommending how aid should be distributed over the coming year. This was then presented to and discussed by the four Under Secretaries who were responsible for implementing the aid programme.

I had noticed the efforts made by my predecessors over the years as they spent days, if not weeks, behind their calculators working out an ideal programme which would benefit the poorest countries and generate economic and social development. The results inevitably recommended that most British aid should be transferred to the Asian sub-continent where need was greatest. This would have entailed a large reduction in aid to our traditional Commonwealth recipients in Africa, which was unrealistic as it would cause massive disruption; and anyhow was not acceptable to the relevant Under Secretary (who was the decision maker).

Determined not to waste either my, or my administrative colleagues', time with unrealistic recommendations my proposals for change were modest and marginal.. Since aid funds overall were increasing it was unlikely that any Under Secretary would accept a reduction in his country programme. I was surprised however, when my very modest changes were rejected by the Under Secretary responsible, and the others stood by him. Increases in aid were allocated on a percentage basis so that as far as Under Secretaries were concerned the allocation was "fair". Not a very convincing way of allocating foreign aid. Although, since most of Britain's aid programme went to poorer Commonwealth countries, the overall allocation was not unreasonable.

Nevertheless there was one geographic area and department, which while not too important in terms of amounts of aid, was not meeting either our development policies or our political policies.

These were the British Dependent Territories which were administered by a joint Foreign Office and Overseas Development Department. They consisted of a large number of tiny islands in the Pacific and Caribbean, plus Gibraltar and the Falkland Islands. They were in receipt of increasingly large amounts of aid per head of population and were becoming more and more dependent economically upon the UK, despite the fact that our policy was to make them more economically and politically independent. Furthermore in real terms they were all quite well off.

At one time or another I had visited all these tiny islands (and Gibraltar) and came to the conclusion that, while statistics suggested they were poor, in fact in real terms, (climate, food, health) they were really quite prosperous, and that our large injections of aid were creating inflationary pressures in the islands and undermining their own development efforts. Admittedly Gibraltar and the Falkland Islands were in a different category and the aid was provided for purely political reasons. This would have been defensible had it not been for the fact that Foreign Office policy was, discreetly, to seek to rid Britain of these two- left over remnants of Empire which were of no strategic or economic value and caused problems with more powerful and valuable neighbours, Spain and Argentina. Providing aid merely encouraged the demand for more aid.

I decided at one of the annual reviews to make my concern clearer to the Under Secretaries and since I was able to set the agenda I ensured that the Foreign Office programme came first. I explained quite clearly that in almost all these cases we were not meeting our policies and just building up dependency relationships. Being realistic I did not suggest a reduction in aid but suggested that it should be frozen at existing levels – rather than increasing it. Much to my amazement my advice was accepted by the majority of Under Secretaries, much to the dismay of the Foreign Office Under Secretary.

Having achieved my modest objectives I supported all the other claims. However, when the Secretary of the Committee who was keeping a check on our decisions added them all up he found that there was an under-spend resulting from my proposals.

"Poor old Ronnie" said our Chairman as he turned to the disconsolate Foreign Office Under Secretary, "What shall we do about your programme ?" "Why do we not restore the cuts ?", said another. The "Barons" all nodded their agreement.

THE WORLD BANK (IBRD)

The appointment of Robert McNamara to head the World Bank in 1972 was in my opinion, far from being a wise liberal step as most thought at the time, but an unmitigated disaster for the Bank.

Robert McNamara was widely regarded as one of the greatest of America's industrial tycoons because he had saved Ford Motors from bankruptcy. His management targets (largely cars per unit factory) were very effective, but when he moved to being the USA's Secretary for Defense, during the Vietnam war, his "bombs per hectare" did not achieve the same success.

When he took up his post at the World Bank he introduced the same form of central "targeting". These were loans per country. Each desk officer for a country was given a target set centrally which he or she was required to meet. These were very closely monitored and desk officers not meeting them were unlikely to prosper in career terms. His great prestige enabled him to secure huge increases in aid for the Bank which was then allocated to countries regardless of their absorptive capacity.

While centrally dreamed up targets are more often than not counterproductive, and could usually be ignored by those dealing with implementation if necessary, in the World Bank McNamara developed one of the earliest computerised systems to check on the performance of desk officers.

I had come across these pressures while serving on World Bank missions in earlier years. On these missions we were constantly reminded by the desk officer that he or she could not go back to Washington without a multi-million dollar project. So when preparing rural development projects, and in particular loans to farmers, it was quite easy to increase the overall amount of the loan by including larger numbers of farmers. If one was proposing, say, a $500 loan to a farmer, one could easily design a loan for many thousands of farmers. Whether there was the administrative ability or the institutions in the country to be able to manage such large loans was seldom taken into account.

At the time McNamara took over the Bank there was a widely held academic view that free-market economics had failed the poor and that "trickledown" was not sufficient (although there was no evidence that there was any better system), and that more direct forms of aid to assist them were necessary. One of the main instruments of this policy in the World Bank was a new Rural Development Department. The British agricultural advisers were ousted and a very able, pleasant American Agricultural Economist became Head of the Department (by extraordinary coincidence he had been the person who, when visiting Rhodesia 15 years previously had recommended me to the United Nations in Ethiopia – obviously a highly intelligent individual).

The decision to expand the activities of the Agricultural Department in the Bank had much merit but the targets set for expenditure led to the preparation of masses of multi-million- dollar rural development projects all over the world. These not only covered direct aid to farmers but investment in storage, marketing facilities, rural roads and transport, anything associated with agriculture.

There was little wrong with this approach in principle but the sheer scale of the projects required an administrative structure well beyond the capacity of most recipients, many of whom were encountering post-colonial disruption, while being inundated by aid missions.

A number of these reports landed on my desk for comment. They were all in countries in knew well and I recorded that they entailed far more loans than could be sensibly absorbed by farmers and were likely to leave farmers and recipient countries in debt – despite very low interest rates.

I was able to persuade my bosses in London, and the new Director of the Rural Development Division of the World Bank, to allow me to spend a week discussing my doubts with World Bank Officials. I flew over and met all the senior Agricultural Advisers advising on Africa, and then their country Directors. The former all agreed that the agricultural projects were far too optimistic but their superior administrative officers disagreed. When I put my conclusions to the Director, that I thought that many of the projects were likely to fail, he did not disagree but argued that all the ancillary infrastructure in roads, marketing facilities, etc. would be a benefit. Not in my view a convincing answer.

It was only some ten years later after innumerable evaluations of agricultural projects that the Bank belatedly reached the same conclusion. Most had failed.

The Bank has been freed from national quotas for recruitment which other United Nations organisations require, (meaning that nationality rather than competence was the principal criteria for staff appointment), and this has enabled it to recruit some of the best brains in the world, at huge salaries, and fund some excellent research. However, its development achievements have been modest and often counterproductive due to the relentless pressure placed upon staff to meet arbitrarily imposed centrally determined, targets.

On one occasion the Bank informed member countries that their annual contributions had to increase by 20%. This caused great concern in our Ministry as our funds for the year were fully committed. When consulted about the Bank's claim I looked into it and found that the Bank was expecting huge increases in their country programmes in the coming year. In the case of their Indian aid programme it was planned to increase it by around 50%. In my view this was quite ridiculous and once more I was despatched to Washington to discuss their demands.

The Head of Finance at the Bank arranged for me to meet some key desk officers to discuss these plans. I vividly recall meeting their Indian desk officer who managed their largest programme, a pleasant American woman. I asked her "Can you increase your spending on India next year by 50% ?" "Of course not," she replied. "But it is in your next year's budget that you will." "This is news to me, and quite impossible to achieve", she adamantly replied.

I returned to see the Finance Officer and informed him of this response, which was similar to that of other desk officers I had met. He airily replied, "We never consult desk officers, as they always get it wrong."

This was a rather tricky situation as we were legally obliged to contribute our share to the Bank and how could they admit that their claims were nonsense? I then realised that we might have another very simple solution. Our Ministry financial year ended on the fifth of April, the Bank's on the last day of June. If we delayed our payment by a month we would fall into our next financial year, but still be within the Bank's financial year. When I proposed this solution to the Finance Officer his reply was "No problem".

When I returned to London with this very simple solution they could not believe that there was such a simple answer and I was sent back again with an Administrative colleague to formally agree this delay.

It is true that this only postponed the problem for a year, but alas, for reasons set out later, I was unable to take part in negotiations which could have come up with a better long term solution.

THE EUROPEAN COMMUNITY

When Britain joined the European Community in 1975, I was detailed to lead a small Mission of professionals to visit Brussels and to assess the EC aid programme.

Our unanimous conclusions were that they were woefully understaffed to carry out the large aid programme they had to implement, and they had neither the skills nor experience to manage it.

Over the following years it was one of my Division's roles to send over an economist once a month to sit on the Projects Committee which approved EC aid. I would frequently go over, or brief the staff who did. The projects submitted to the Committee were invariably of very poor quality and I doubt whether 75% of them would have been approved had they been submitted for approval to our Projects Committee. However, on the EC Projects Committee we had a weighted vote, 28%, as did the French and the Germans. The representatives of these two countries were firmly under control of their Foreign Office and never dared turn a project down, so we were always out-voted, regardless of the awfulness of the project.

Some of the apparently least harmful EC projects were road projects. We let them through without objection as we deemed them the least harmful, despite the fact that most of them were unlikely to generate much traffic and required considerable maintenance. Years later I benefited from driving along a splendid EC- funded tarmac road from Addis Ababa, Ethiopia, to the Kenyan frontier. It was a splendidly comfortable and speedy journey as we were one of the very few vehicles on the road but we could not help noticing that inadequate maintenance meant that grass was growing over parts of the road and that untended gullies were undermining it.

Sadly, the EC aid programme was the most inefficient of all the aid programmes I had encountered. Too much aid, too few staff, too few skilled staff and too many staff members who regarded themselves as there to represent the interests of their native country rather than that of the EC. The allocation of aid was 100% political and decisions, to an increasing extent, needed to be audited but were not.

ONE DOOR CLOSES

Few of us in the Economic Planning Staff were surprised to learn in the early Thatcher years that there was to be a review of the senior management of our Service. It had been very obvious for years that we were top heavy. There was a Director General (Deputy Secretary), a Deputy Director General (Under Secretary), and three Directors (ranked between Assistant Secretary and Under Secretary) of which I was one.

For years the Deputy post had been filled by eminent and itinerant academics who laboured behind calculators or produced voluminous reports which no one read. The post was clearly redundant. It was at that time filled by a pleasant Cambridge trained Foreign Office economist who had no development experience and had not ventured overseas beyond Monte Carlo. He was always available for a chat and I am eternally grateful for him for urging me to read "Nostromo" by Joseph Conrad, but never, in the years I had been his subordinate had he ever become involved in my work or that of my Division.

It was the accepted wisdom by everyone (apart presumably from the incumbent) that this post was superfluous. The three of us who were Directors could then, with a minor upgrade to Under Secretary equivalent, provide for a more cost- effective administration.

But it is curious how reason does not always prevail. In fact the management review, carried out by what seemed to us Directors, as junior administrators, was a surprise, if not a shock, as it came to the conclusion that our three Director posts should be abolished. How they came to reach this bizarre conclusion was never clear. Maybe they got a performance award for number of posts abolished ? Maybe the Foreign Office was determined to keep its "outpost" in place. We never saw the report or ever received an explanation for this decision.

Having just returned from Washington, having solved a tricky budgetary World Bank problem and my jointly published book having received good reviews, one could not help but feel that justice, let alone competence, had not been high in the minds of those making the decision.

Once recovered from the surprise, and discovering that the recommendation was supported by one's superiors, I became interested in the compensation package. This was extremely attractive. I would be offered my pension straight away plus eight added years which would take me up to the age at which I would have had to retire anyway. On top of that, there was a lump sum compensation which would enable me to purchase that beautifully located flat, overlooking St.Ives harbour, in Cornwall, which Jean was keen on. The offer seemed to be too good to be true. At the same time the job, after nearly 20 years, was becoming rather repetitive as every five years the same old rejected projects and ideas came up and we were under pressure to spend more and more aid regardless of the fact that there were fewer needy recipients, fewer deserving governments and far more aid donors competing to give away money. I reckoned that with a couple of days consultancy work per week I would readily make up my salary loss and it would give me time for other activities.

While I was sorry to leave what had been an excellent organisation with competent, well-motivated colleagues it did seem to be time to move on.

ANOTHER DOOR OPENS

The Crown Agents had been the administrative arm of the Colonial Service. In colonial days it recruited staff, paid them, purchased all colonial governments' requirements, invested their reserves and generally provided all the backup services they required.

As overseas governments became independent, the Crown Agents had been obliged to become more entrepreneurial and compete for work with international agencies with whom they quickly established a reputation for integrity and competence.

They offered me a couple of days consultancy per week to build up an economics consultancy department. I was allowed total freedom to determine my work pattern provided I brought in sufficient income to cover my costs. I was able to do this very quickly and with some very able young staff – an administrator and an economist built up a unit which had teams of economists working in Uganda, Fiji, Papua New Guinea, Somalia, all funded by the World Bank, the EC or the UN. We were eventually bringing in close on £1m a year for the Crown Agents, several times more than our annual costs.

This part-time job was extremely stimulating as, having always worked within the security of the public sector, it was the first time, working in a very competitive private sector, I had to go and sell my services in order to justify my salary. Marketing one's services was sometimes embarrassing or even humiliating if rejected, but winning contracts against stiff international competition was very satisfying. One learned that one could survive in the "real" competitive world in which most people worked.

This part-time job enabled me to devote more time to local issues in Guildford and I was persuaded to stand as a candidate for the Liberal Democrats in the Ward where I lived in 1983. However, it was a ward which the Conservatives had held for many years and insufficient numbers of the electorate were persuaded to shift their allegiances for such a splendid candidate and my first electoral attempt ended in failure.

Chapter Eleven

A "STATION" FOR THE SULTAN

"Do you think you can do it?" said the Chairman. "It's a tricky assignment and we cannot afford to get it wrong - he is our best client – it will be like walking on eggs."

The Chief Executive of the Crown Agents, the large, ex- colonial administrative support unit, who had offered me two days work per week, had asked me earlier whether I would go to Australia with a surveyor they had appointed to buy a station for the Sultan of Brunei.

"Buy a station?" I responded with surprise "I've never been in the rail business, and certainly not in Australia."

"In Australia", the Chief Executive explained patiently," a station is a cattle ranch not a railway station, and the Sultan wants to buy one as his meat supplies from Australia have been interrupted and he thinks that he can secure a reliable supply if he owns a station."

Seeing the look of astonishment on my face he went on, "We have located an expert who knows cattle and Australia who is working for surveyors (he named one of the largest Estate Agents in Britain) who we would send out with you. But we also need to send someone who can represent us and ensure that we recommend a suitable property at the best price." He tactfully did not mention that it would also justify the fee they would charge.

It certainly sounded an attractive proposition but had I the qualifications for what could be a tricky assignment? It is surprising how quickly one can find reasons for justifying a decision, despite the fact that I had never been to Australia and I had never been involved in purchasing any real estate, let alone a ranch. I desperately ransacked past memories. I had purchased my house, but this hardly qualified me as an expert in buying an Australian "station". I then recalled that I had helped round up cattle during my school holidays on my uncle's ranch in Argentina. More relevantly I had carried out costings of European- owned ranches in Rhodesia, and I had written an article for a United Nations bulletin on "Livestock Policies in Latin America". Even better I had been on a World Bank Livestock Mission to Uruguay which eventually led to a multi-million dollar loan being made to that country. And on top of that, investment analysis was my forte. Not exactly ideal qualifications for the purpose but surely I could not let the organisation down and refuse the offer? "Right" I said, "You can depend on me."

The organisation I was working for had served, generally competently and honestly, all the colonial administrations of the Empire, but as countries became independent many new Governments had succumbed to the enticements of private enterprise predators who ensured that their new clients did not go unrewarded, and the work of the Crown Agents had diminished alarmingly.

The Sultan with his massive oil wealth had most of his financial portfolio, running into hundreds of millions of pounds, managed by the Crown Agents, and was thus a vitally important client. Any wish of his needed to be dealt with efficiently and speedily, however unusual it might be.

This was why, no doubt, I sat in the Chairman's lush office and was assessed as to whether they could afford to let me loose on this mission. But since they needed a presence on the mission and I was the best they had, my assurances that I could cope were accepted.

The organisation had already sent out the surveyor to Australia to draw up a short list and my function, together with two representatives from Brunei, was to go out to Darwin in northern Australia and choose the best "station".

I eventually arrived at Darwin, a clean, modern one-storey town, with wide, empty avenues, on an early winter morning with temperature at an all-time low of 30 degrees. Everyone was incredibly young; all the men dressed in shorts with long ex-colonial-style stockings, and the incredibly attractive girls in the skimpiest clothes one could imagine. There was a complete absence of old people, an absence I commented on to the Chief Planner next day. He agreed and said it was his big problem everyone was too young. Apart from assuring me we could purchase a station, he asked if we could help resolve their age problem. As Britain had more than its fair share of experienced grey hairs I promised to consider this.

At the hotel I met up with Reg, my fellow Brit, who was the cattle purchasing expert, Norman, another Brit who was a vet from Brunei. and Datta who was responsible for agriculture in Brunei.

I cannot say my companions gave me much confidence. Datta, a diminutive little man, never said a word, and Norman who looked like a shifty refugee from a Humphrey Bogart film, smoked wispy hand-rolled cigarettes which hung precariously from his lower lip, and who informed us early on that he had shares in a brothel in the Philippines. This remarkable piece of information was a conversation stopper as we pondered how the annual accounts were prepared and how his share of his investment was verified.

However, the key man was Reg. He came from one of the English border counties and would clearly have been in his element at a rural county agricultural show in an immaculate tweed suit and shooting cap. He told me that in fact he did attend many shows, as he was a "foxhound" judge. I had hoped that he would say that he was a cattle judge, but it was not to be. One wondered what Aussie ranchers would make of him. Fortunately he had abandoned his tweedy, county attire for something sartorially more appropriate to the outback.

We assembled early next morning to carry out our survey. A small private aircraft awaited us and the four of us squeezed in beside a cheery Aussie pilot. Norman looked exceptionally poorly. It turned out that those friendly languorous lassies draped around the hotel swimming pool were not air hostesses at all but ladies of easy but expensive virtue. Norman had spent the night with one and found that he had to fork out £100 for the experience – 100 times more than similar facilities in the Philippines and, almost as bad, costing the equivalent of four days hotel expenses. I do not think he ever recovered from the shock, as he never spoke again.

Reg then told us that he had already picked a property which he thought was the best one. It was by then too late, as the propeller ticked over, to protest and say that I thought we were to assess several stations; certainly not in front of our Brunei colleagues. Anyhow how on earth was I going to compare miles and miles of scrubby Australian properties, they would all look the same.

So we set off over miles and miles of tiny bushes scattered in a semi-desert landscape and eventually sought to land on a smooth piece of ground, which we identified as an airstrip as it had a limp weather sock at one end. Unfortunately it was populated by huge evil-looking bustards. Since there was no one to chase them away our pilot had to do this by zooming over them. This seemed a little rash to me, as there was no accounting for the direction in which these beastly birds fly, but he was eventually successful, though one wild panic stricken bird brushed past our cabin window.

The station, which had been selected, covered 1.5 million acres. Yes, I will repeat it: 1.5 million acres. It was owned by Luke a tall rangy American from Montana, who together with about twenty others from that State had come to grow corn on an immense scale a few years earlier – but they had all failed. For those old enough to recall the British Government's disastrous groundnuts scheme in Tanganyika in 1948, this novel disaster reminded one that not only State enterprises failed.

But Luke had built himself a nice house, with a swimming pool and an open-air cinema screen, and a whole complex of houses on stilts with large verandas protected by mosquito netting for his now non-existent staff. We decided to visit where his foreman lived, it was 70 miles, yes, 70 miles away.

Luke told us that he had about 25,000 to 35,000 cattle on his station, some 10,000 donkeys and about 1,500 wild horses.

While we were there, cattle were rounded up for examination and herded into corrals. But not by cowboys –but by helicopters. Two of them buzzed between the scrubby trees and chased the stock around. I was offered a chance to fly in one but decided that my family might miss me if one of the rotor blades came off.

Having seen the property and being able to substantiate its existence and its physical assets, we flew back to Darwin. Reg recommended we should purchase it. There did not seem much option.

The next big decision was how much were we going to offer? I asked Reg what he thought. He was very canny and refused to suggest a figure and asked me for my views. Meanwhile he was busy with innumerable callers and visitors all trying to flog off other "useless" stations, or so he described them. But he refused to tell me what the property was worth or what we should offer.

This was a tricky situation for me. How were we to explain to the Sultan that the price we had negotiated was a reasonable one? What if we offered far too much? Could we be accused of taking a rake-off?

Fortunately, when with the World Bank I had learned how to carry out financial appraisals of cattle projects so I decided that I had better do one on this project. To do this one needs a large sheet of paper and to make a forecast for the next twenty years of the number of cows, their calving rates, the calf-survival rate, death rates, age at sale, weight at sale and probable sale price. Then one makes some equally arbitrary assumptions about annual costs, quite low except for helicopters, and the final column gives one the net surplus every year.

Since this exercise in futurology only gives one a flow of future surpluses, one has to convert these figures by what is called discounting, that is bringing them all back to a present value by using an interest rate. It is in fact the reverse of compound interest.

In those days without computers it was laborious task. I was working happily away at these notional sheets of figures when my calculator gave up the ghost. Battery exhausted. Nightmare – how could I justify my mission? It would take days to do it all by hand. So I rushed out into the deserted Darwin streets to find a battery. None available. However, I eventually found a shop with a battery.

I completed my forecasts of the economic value though I made quite a number of assumptions, so I set a minimum and maximum value. These came out at between £2m and £3m.

I explained all this to Reg and asked him what his figure was. "About the same as yours," he said. I was not sure whether to feel flattered or suspicious but he said that he was fairly certain that the sellers would accept this figure.

I did press him to let me know how he calculated his estimate of the value of the "station". After all what if the Sultan wanted to know how we had calculated the price? However he refused to tell me, saying, " If I tell them how I worked out the value then next time they would be able to do it themselves and they would not need to use me." My suspicion, since confirmed by working with other surveyors, is that he had no method but just responded to sales brochures - less 10%.

The sellers settled for £3m and we decided to head to Brunei with the good news.

On the way back our Brunei colleagues turned on me – Reg was on a separate flight from us, and said that they should have been given a greater choice and they knew of a cheaper alternative. They had a point but it was rather late to raise it. Controlling my panic as we would look very silly if they decided to denounce us for incompetence or worse when we got to Brunei, I assured them that Reg had looked at many options. When we met up with Reg, he asked them what station they were thinking of and, truthfully or not, said that it was not for sale. This shut them up.

Brunei is a tiny enclave of about 120,000 people on one of Indonesia's larger islands, and its wealth showed in the form of a superb artificial lake surrounded by mosques and magnificent polo grounds. The Sultan was shrewd enough to ensure that some of his immense wealth provided a decent standard of living for his subjects, and the town was an attractive well-planned and prosperous haven, though one wondered what they made of his plans to build a palace capable of entertaining 6,000 guests.

We had an audience planned with the Prime Minister so I thought that we had better have a meeting with our dissatisfied colleagues first, but Reg insisted this was not necessary. I was somewhat dubious about this but the Prime Minister, when we were ushered into his lavish presence, showed no interest in the £3m price, which was probably equivalent to a couple of hours' oil revenue, and only wanted to be assured that their meat needs would be met. He particularly wanted to know whether the station was larger than that of the neighbouring Sultan of Sarawak. It was – indeed it was bigger than Brunei itself. He then told his Director of Agriculture to go away and produce a report confirming the purchase of the station. Reg was right.

We later appointed an Australian management company to run the station and about a year later when I met the Chairman I enquired as to the success of our Mission.

"No broken eggs," he said.

Chapter Twelve

MAYOR OF GUILDFORD

There are two ways of becoming Mayor of a town. The easy way and the hard way. One has, of course, to be an elected councillor to become a Mayor. But once elected, it is then just a matter of waiting until one's time comes up – as Mayors are usually chosen by length of service.

The easy way to get elected is to chose a political party which has a comfortable majority and be prepared to stand in whichever ward that party has a majority. Preferably choose a multi-candidate ward where there are several councillors as this means there is a better chance of being selected. Political parties are usually pretty short of willing candidates and it should not be that difficult, provided one's sympathies are with that political party, to get selected and then elected. Once elected any moderately conscientious councillor should be able to retain the seat for a few years, and then become Mayor.

The hard way is to select a ward in which there is a councillor with whose views you do not agree and stand against him – or her. This means that one has to oust a sitting elected Member

I chose the "hard way". I lived in one of the most attractive wards which covered the fine old Tudor town centre, with some beautiful leafy suburbs and popular open spaces on the slopes of the North Downs. By attachment and contacts therefore this was the only ward I would wish to represent. Unfortunately it already had a councillor – a popular Conservative Councillor and Conservatives had represented the ward for what seemed forever. The problem for me was that I was not conservative, I was a Liberal. Although in the work of a councillor national party politics are of little importance, as one is concerned with day-to- day problems of the constituents of one's ward, come election time, unfortunately, most voters are very much influenced by national politics and use local elections as a proxy Gallup poll and will vote accordingly. Furthermore in order to get elected the administrative support of a national party is invaluable.

As one may imagine, trying to unseat a Conservative was no easy task. However while Guildford is perceived nationally as a smug, comfortable, conservative, commuter community, it has in fact a high percentage of blue- collar workers, and a very high percentage of middle- class professionals. It is not as conservative as it seems. Neither do commuters dominate the economy, for it is fact extremely diversified and one of the key centres of economic growth in Britain. It has an impressive range of high- tech enterprises – mini space satellites, computers, motor vehicles, as well as an impressive science-based University. In fact, it is a centre of world excellence in many economic and social fields.

Having been at the forefront of many community activities for nearly a decade, I naively thought that standing against a well-established Conservative in 1983 was worth doing despite the warning from a friendly, feisty, lady Conservative Councillor " Mr Bridger – in your ward, if they put up a blue stick as a councillor, it would win" She was right. Not that a stick got voted in but the Conservative held his seat.

Ever determined, I stood again four years later. This time I thought I had a very good chance as the well known Conservative Councillor had retired and their new candidate was an outsider, from the neighbouring rival town of Woking. Did I get in? Not at all.

However, it had been drummed into me by my mother, who was a Bruce and claimed descent from that most famous of all Scottish kings, that " if you fail, try, try and try again" So in 1991 I stood once again. This time the gods or King Bruce were on my side for both I and my colleague (it was a two seat ward) replaced the Conservatives.

I stood three more times, being re-elected on each occasion , until I decided that 16 years of community service was a reasonable length of time and following in the steps of Voltaire's Candide, who, having become disillusioned with his attempts to save the world, then turned to saving his community.

SIXTEEN YEARS SERVICE

Sixteen years is a substantial slice of one's life. Were all those meetings one had to attend, Planning, Community, Finance, full Council, innumerable reports and minutes one had to read and digest, all those speeches one had to prepare and the arguments and battles over developments - worthwhile ? On top of that one had to keep in touch with one's constituents, produce regular newssheets, get them delivered and at election time embark on a flurry of visits to prospective supporters as well as attend Liberal Party meetings and events.

It is perhaps worth stressing that although from time to time some bitter disputes broke out at Council meetings between the different political groups, and they were almost entirely Liberal and Conservative, (the Labour Group almost disappearing), most Council meetings were conducted in a rational and even good humoured fashion. Political banter was normally good natured and not taken all that seriously as all but a few realised that the issues we dealt with most of the time had no political content.

Fortunately the Council was efficiently run, especially in respect to Housing, Finance and Planning and there were virtually no staff scandals. As for elected representatives, the picture which our national press paints of a venal, corrupt, incompetent self-seeking political class, is one which I do not recognise. As locally elected councillors, foot soldiers of the political class which rules the country, I can only say that the vast majority did their best to serve their community. However, much the tabloid newspapers seek to discredit elected representatives almost all those I have met and worked with are not recognisable as portrayed by most of the national press. Furthermore, having worked and travelled abroad one can only be impressed by the way Government works in Britain and the quality of the vast majority of elected of representatives.

Looking back at sixteen years " hard labour", which usually entailed attending three or four meetings a week, reading large numbers of sometimes very complex reports and attending to constituents complaints, one often wonders what one achieved. Was it all worthwhile ?

The major problem of assessing one's contribution is that in most cases there is a collective decision, and claiming credit for a Council action can be presumption and challenged by others who may claim the idea was theirs. The introduction of CCTV, for example, is an interesting case in point. Having read of its successful use in various towns in Britain I collected examples of these reports and even a video of how it was used in King's Lynn, produced a short report for colleagues and copied it to the Police. The Police were interested and a Committee was set up. The Police had not got the funds to purchase the capital equipment but said they would run it if the Council provided the hardware. This we agreed to do. Eventually forty- five cameras were installed and these were a great success. Several libertarian councillors who had opposed this "appalling intrusion on our lives" were soon demanding cameras for their wards. Does one claim this as a personal achievement ? It would have come anyhow – if perhaps a few years later.

However, the greatest resistance to any new ideas came not from other councillors but from staff. It is alas generally true that new ideas are other people's ideas to those who need to implement them, and are almost always resented and resisted by those responsible. Added to this most civil servants rather resent and resist elected "amateurs" telling them what they should do. They assume that they know what needs to be done rather than politicians who all too often are seen as being only concerned with short- term electoral gain. There is some truth in this assessment, as an elected representative cannot ignore the electoral consequences of their decisions. Alas this is what democracy is about. Nevertheless, I found it surprising that so many of what were, in my view, reasonable improvements were resisted.

Perhaps the most important quality one requires when working in the public sector, (and it is important to work with officers instead of against them, as they have immense power to ensure things do not get done) is perseverance.

One proposal I made for a pedestrian crossing joining up two sections of the High Street, which had been cut by a major road, took five years to get accepted. It took six years to get a small extension of the pedestrianised High Street to be carried out. Another safer road crossing was one Jean had petitioned for twenty years and it took me, when I became a Councillor, nearly ten years to get it implemented.

Another interesting example of the power of reluctant officials to implement reasonable (to councillors) proposals was related to the property portfolio. Guildford, as I soon discovered had a huge, diversified commercial property portfolio. The Council owned shops, garages, farms, offices and houses. When I asked to see a list I was told there was not one. The officers then claimed that councillors could not see it as it contained confidential information. Exasperated I then proposed a motion to the Council that we should publish a list of our commercial property. This was agreed. Even then it took another two years before it was published. Even when it was published and I urged some members of the public to ask for it they were grilled by officers as to why they needed to see it. There was a deeply held belief by officers that councillors could not be trusted and if they knew of the vast amount of "family silver" the Council owned there would be a sales carnival.

.This attitude also carried over to finance, which was a very efficient Department , but Treasurers everywhere love to squirrel away funds and can become quite neurotic if anyone should wish to dig into their hard acquired reserves. Because of my background I took a special interest in finance and was Chairman of the Finance Committee for a while. I was quite surprised to find that not all the Council's financial reserves were in the Estimates Book, which were the ones councillors examined, but in Audited Accounts which councillors never read. Officers must have been surprised that I actually spent time trying to understand this document, and especially why there were nearly £4m recorded as reserves, which were not in the Estimates we had approved. The explanation I received was confused, but next year £4m appeared in the Estimate Book. Several other suggestions which I made to improve presentation of estimates, which were sometimes disputed by officers (often quite reasonably), would appear a year or so later.

Planning was another major Committee which caused many problems and much excitement. Sitting on this Committee was quite rewarding as one could influence decisions quite significantly as planning policies are so many, so vague and often contradictory, that well- reasoned arguments could lead to a decision different from the one that Planning Officers recommended. This responsibility did not however, come without a cost, as a controversial decision meant upsetting as well as pleasing someone, and although one can confidently say that planning decisions were always free of any illegal pressures this did not stop disaffected members of the public challenging one's integrity. Fortunately this only occurred to me on two occasions in sixteen years of public service. The first was when a disaffected residents chalked on a wall "Bridger is a crook", as I had approved s planning application many had objected to. On the second occasion when some unpleasant residents complained to the Standards Committee that I had taken coffee with the Headmaster of the local school who were asking for planning permission for a development they objected to as they saw this as my being influenced unfairly by the applicant.

There were many minor schemes, such as planting and landscaping, better sign posting, tree planting, extension of the pedestrian areas, introduction of street cafe policy, which one was responsible for suggesting and which from time to time seemed to justify one's time and effort.

There were a few years when we Liberals ran the Council, and Guildford of all places even elected a Liberal Member of Parliament; and these were fruitful years. My greatest and unrecognised achievement, and with critical help of the Treasurer, was to set a budget which was lower than the year before. This had never been done in living memory. It was coincidence of course that it was election year. Alas this splendid feat was never recognised as the Guildford Budget is only 10% of the total Council budget which covered the Surrey County Council and the Police, so no one noticed this stupendous achievement.

Eventually we Liberals lost control of the Council to Conservatives and then Government reformed the way Councils were managed giving power to a small coterie of councillors via an Executive committee, on the grounds that this would lead to more effective governance. What it did in practice was to make the majority of councillors feel less empowered, and gave so much work to a few who served on the Executive committee, that it effectively meant that officials made more of the decisions.

So as old age approached, and there was a possibility of standing as Mayor before I retired, I threw my hat in the ring, and it was agreed by my colleagues that I should be proposed for this very ancient role. Which I was and was elected.

MAYOR OF GUILDFORD

The origin of the Mayoralty of Guildford disappears into the mists of medieval time. There are 443 Mayors recorded on a scroll in the seventeenth century Borough Guildhall, but there have been more.

The fine timbered Court rooms and Mayor's parlour have been an important meeting place for many centuries. The Municipal silver collection, which includes a Mayoral staff given by Queen Elizabeth the First, is one of the finest in the country. The Mayor's gold chain of office was given to the Borough in 1673.

Over time, rituals have been created and the Mayor, Aldermen and Councillors on important events and on civic parades dress in red and black coloured robes wearing tri- corned hats. Having to open the annual pantomime I appeared in full Mayoral dress on the stage and stated " I am not part of the pantomime." "Oh yes you are," the children roared back.

The Mayor presides over full Council meetings but otherwise plays little part in the Council decision making process as the role is non-political and representational. The latter is a demanding one, even frenetic sometimes when five events are scheduled for one day, and over the year the Mayor could attend up to 700 events. These include Boy Scouts AGMs, important meetings of the multitude of charities who carry out splendid social work in the community, opening fetes, attending prize givings, church services, concerts, lectures, theatres, visiting old people's homes, welcoming important visitors including royalty, planting trees, opening new buildings, giving out awards as well as supporting charities and, by custom, promoting a theme for the year.

My theme was "Guildford – a centre of world excellence". Its purpose being to make more people appreciate that Guildford was not just a smug, prosperous Conservative, commuter enclave as often proposed by the media, but was a world leader in such fields as mini satellites (there are 25 circling the earth,), a centre of computer technology (the home of Alan Turing and a centre for computer games), the largest centre for training in Britain for keyhole surgery, a major international centre for sleep research, and a manufacturer of specialised motor vehicles. With the help of the university we organised a series of public lectures which were attended by up to 300 people.

Taking on the Mayoralty effectively ties one down for the whole year and allows time for few other activities. This demanding role, combined with the custom that the Mayor should not become involved in politics, means that there are councillors who prefer not to offer themselves for the honour of being elected as Mayor.

The task is however, is made much easier by the provision of a first-class Secretary, a splendid singing Custodian of the Guildhall and a cheerful chauffeur who never gets lost and always arrives in time, in the Mayor's large, immaculately polished Jaguar car.

As one discovers, being invited to all these events gives one a splendid insight into the immense and varied community activities of those living in the Borough. One cannot speak highly enough of the selfless dedication of people who organise such varied charitable work. Apart from the many groups for the elderly and the young, there are sports organisations, health charities, fund- raising committees, churches, environment groups, gardening organisations, musical societies, theatrical groups, educational groups. They all provide the "glue" which enables a society which has reorganised itself spatially and socially, severing age old family ties, to function with new links for support and development.

Guildford has been fortunate in providing a wide range of educational and cultural activities, and as Mayor one was invited to preside over or attend events by the excellent Council Philharmonic Orchestra, superb performances by the many local choirs, theatrical events at the splendid Yvonne Arnaud Theatre , as well a rich array of very talented amateur theatrical and musical events.

In summer there were Garden Parties, the most prestigious being the one at Buckingham Palace, though this was somewhat marred by having to share the Queen with 8,000 other guests – but the tea and cakes were of very high quality - and who minds waiting an hour or so in a queue to get into the Palace ?

SPEECHMAKING

At many of these events one had to make a speech. One was always given a briefing note which stated exactly who was to meet one, who they were whether food was provided, whether a speech was required and how long one should stay. Fortunately Jean usually accompanied me and helped ensure that we socialised usefully.

On one occasion I lost my briefing note when I was to give out Government Awards for Export Promotion at the local hotel. I could not understand how a hotel could get an award for exports ? Were they exporting hotels nowadays? How could they do it? I was puzzling this over and wondering how I should congratulate the assembled group of well-dressed young executives for their achievements. Maybe they were dealing in Tourism and tourism is a sort of export – in reverse. Also present was the High Sheriff of Surrey and various other notables, and when I made a brief speech about their great contribution to exports I thought I had better congratulate the hotel and the hotel trade for their efforts. I detected from some uneasy eye shifting responses that maybe I had got it wrong. The applause on completion was muted but polite. Going round congratulating those present after the speech I discovered to my surprised embarrassment that they were all computer specialists and had nothing to do with the hotel trade. Could have been worse I suppose.

I had expected that visiting homes for the elderly might be quite a chore and that it could be rather depressing to see how these sad, neglected, elderly lived. Both Jean and I were quite surprised to find that almost every home we visited seemed to be teeming with lively, very happy people. Admittedly the survival rates of women are greater and they dominated, but they all seemed very jolly. They enjoyed excellent facilities, they had the privacy in their own apartments and could socialise as much as they wanted. Their Wardens organised outings and house events for them throughout the week. They were, much to our relief, very pleased to meet the Mayor and more so the Mayoress who was especially good at listening to them.

My best social contribution was a brief speech which depended on a couple of jokes for effect. These were: Two old ladies had not seen each other for some time and one asked the other.

"Hullo Mabel, how is George?"
"Oh dear haven't you heard?"
"No. What happened?"
"He went out to pick some beans for dinner in the garden and died""
"You poor thing. What did you do?"
"Oh ! I had to open a tin of peas"

Another one, which Jean tried to stop me telling as she thought it rather rude went as follows:
Two old men friends meet: "George, why are you wearing that suppository in your ear ?"
"Oh my God ! Where have I put my hearing aid?"

Other speeches were more demanding. The most important being at the Annual Dinner of the Governing Body of the University of Surrey. This was a sumptuous formal meeting (dinner jackets), with all the great and good of academia. As Mayor, I had to make a speech of welcome. This did not seem to be an occasion for a jokey introduction, although I wondered what previous Mayors had said. It occurred to me that my speech might contain a few helpful thoughts about what had gone wrong with university education. Why was Britain not producing the great engineering giants of the nineteenth century – Brunel, Watts, etc. They might even find my speech of great value. The essence of it would be that since then, engineers and scientists had gone to Universities where they had been taught academic purity and to look down on commerce and industry and the pursuit of private profit. This argument might disturb some of those present and might even interrupt the consumption of their desserts and make them sit up. Once they had reacted, probably adversely to this argument I would then follow on with, " but Surrey University is different for you have been pioneers in establishing a partnership with commerce and industry" and "your students have an excellent employment record – the best in Britain". Maybe I would get a standing ovation – I would tread where no other Mayor had trod before.

I had the Vice Chancellor on my left, I knew him well and was certain my speech would go down well. On my right I had a stranger. As I chatted to him I discovered he had been Chairman of Britain's largest telecommunication company, Chairman of the Government's Research wards Organisation, Chairman of a large mobile telephone conglomerate, and I suddenly thought that my proposed speech from this "pigmy" Mayor was enormously presumptuous in such august company. What should I do? Should I tear it up and just thank them for a good meal.?

I thought I would ask his advice. But what if he disagreed ? There was no fall back speech. Would he disagree ? I decided it would be prudent and polite to do so. I was much relieved to be told that my general thesis that the gap between academia and commerce was too great in British Universities and that Surrey was a model which others could follow, was one he agreed with. I went ahead with it. I did not get the standing ovation I thought these helpful observations deserved, though at least I was not booed.

FAREWELL

Being Mayor, together with Jean as Mayoress was a splendid opportunity for us to see how a modern community develops new vital social and economic links, and to make a small contribution to its cohesion. Apart from the Mayoral theme, I was able to promote a delightful book of architectural drawings of Guildford, and to establish a "Mayor's Award for Community Service", (a long needed recognition for the splendid work of so many voluntary workers and forty worthy recipients were identified during the year). I also discovered that the Mayor's charity had reserves equal to 10 years of grants and was able to spend on needy causes a significant amount of these unjustified reserves.

After a year of attending over 500 public events both Jean and I were pleased to pass on the honour and responsibility of representing the Borough, to other colleagues.

Chapter Thirteen

REFLECTIONS

Looking back over the last half of the twentieth century one cannot but reflect that it has been an amazing five decades of economic and social change. For the western world, and many other areas, the technological innovations in transport and communications have made the world easily accessible to millions of people. Their standard of living has doubled if not trebled, and life expectancy increased by nearly a third. It is difficult to think of any other period in world history which has witnessed so much positive change. Prosperity may not, if one reads daily newspapers, bring much contentment, but it has enabled people to complain in comfort.

For the world generally a doubling of the population thanks to technological transformation of agricultural food production, has been a massive achievement which, of course, creates new very serious global problems of overpopulation and huge migratory pressures.

Economic and social progress has not been limited to the Western world but has spread to the Middle East and more recently to the Far East, where Japan, Malaysia, Thailand, Taiwan, Singapore, have led the way, and which China, India, and more recently Vietnam, have copied and they are now set to challenge the hegemony of the USA and Europe.

The transformation of the British economy by the often unpopular Margaret Thatcher's market- led strategy has spread and galvanised the energy skills and initiative of millions of people throughout the world. The abandonment of central planning, which led to misallocation of resources, and often allowed corrupt self- seeking power groups to oppress their citizens, has permitted far more freedom and individual initiative to flourish. Liberated from the dead and often corrupt hand of bureaucracy many countries in the world have taken off into sustained growth.

That this release of energy has left many behind is the inevitable price paid for by progress – unfortunately skills, energy, intelligence are not shared out equally and inequality is an inevitable concomitant of economic growth. Adam Smith and Charles Darwin would agree with this proposition. It is for society through redistributive Government polices to ensure a fairer distribution of these gains. There needs however, to be a balance between stimulating economic efficiency and establishing a more equitable society. This requires good governance.

Many of the "new" countries which have successfully liberalised their economies, such as China, Russia and India, have a long way to go to establish a fairer or democratic society, but there are few who would doubt that even partial liberalisation has been a huge improvement on their previous oppressive, inefficient, governments.

Sadly, much of Africa has not benefited in the years since de-colonisation and many if not most, countries have collapsed or become incorrigibly corrupt. Loyalties are personal, family, or tribal, and not to the nation as a whole. For too many politicians and civil servants the State is there to be plundered – the concept of public service little known, good governance impossible.

Noble attempts to assist countries, particularly in Africa, through providing ever larger quantities of aid when their governance and policies do not provide the conditions for growth, merely ensure that essential reforms are discouraged and support incompetent and dishonest ruling cliques.

The historic lesson of foreign aid is that development is something which must be generated within countries through effort, energy, stability, appropriate policies and a reasonable level of governance. Under these circumstances foreign aid can make a useful marginal difference. Other than in emergencies it should be accepted that in an international age where countries collapse, there is little that outsiders can do or are prepared to do where there is chaos and Kalashnikovs. China, ultimately, learned how to feed its starving masses itself.

My personal odyssey, from my departure from Buenos Aires to retirement in Guildford, was not one I, or indeed anyone, could have forecast. My journey through many countries led me to abandon the widespread post war belief that socialist central planning was the solution to economic and social problems. However, the new liberal market system has created two serious problems, that of income inequality and reckless mis-investment, which only capable government and wise international institutions are likely to be able to resolve.

My experience in local government was that it is perfectly possible to secure improvements to one's environment and one's community but it requires incredible perseverance. With time pressing hard on my heels I felt it should pass on the baton and allow younger more dynamic representatives to replace me. Like Candide I decided to retire and "cultivate my garden".

Printed in the United Kingdom
by Lightning Source UK Ltd.
131285UK00001B/133-189/P